A "CLOZE" LOOK AT ENGLISH

THELMA L. BORODKIN, Ph.D.

Lehman College
City University of New York

HEINLE & HEINLE PUBLISHERS
A Division of Wadsworth, Inc.
Boston, Massachusetts 02116

W/D

*To my dearest husband Sol
and in memory of Carlos A. Yorio*

Cloze passages for Units 1, 3, 4, 5, 6, 7, 8, 9 adapted from *Intermediate Stories for Composition* by Leslie Hill and Prema Popkin (1967) by permission of Oxford University Press. © Oxford University Press 1967.

Text and Cover Design: Suzanne Bennett & Associates
Illustrations: Carol Ann Gaffney

A "Cloze" Look at English

Heinle & Heinle Publishers is a division of Wadsworth, Inc.

Manufactured in the United States of America.

Library of Congress Cataloging-in-Publication data

Borodkin, Thelma L.
    A "cloze" look at English / Thelma L. Borodkin.
        p.   cm.
    ISBN 0-8384-3010-4
    1. English language — Textbooks for foreign speakers.   I. Title.
PE1128.B63   1992
428.2'4 — dc20   91-27451
                                                                                  CIP

ISBN 0-8384-3010-4

10   9   8   7   6   5   4   3   2   1

CONTENTS

TO THE TEACHER

This book has been designed to maximize your creativity as well as that of your students as the latter undertake the task of becoming users of a second language at the college level. In addition to improving language proficiency, the plan of the book is to encourage students to develop those characteristics that distinguish them as good language learners as well as to introduce students to a variety of cognitive learning strategies that will allow them to play a more active role in their second language acquisition process.

Current research on good language learners reveals that such learners share certain characteristics: Good language learners, for example, are characterized by their willingness to take a risk at erring by experimenting with different linguistic forms and by using any and all opportunities for practice. The use of the DRTA (Directed Reading and Thinking Activity, explained below) and the cloze encourages students to develop the cognitive learning strategies of guessing, inferencing, integrating, clarifying, verifying, and rereading, and the metacognitive strategies of predicting, planning, and proving.

Furthermore, there are exercises designed to utilize the collaborative learning mode of instruction as students together discuss their ideas both in a larger, whole-class group and in smaller groups. Students learn how to help one another as they collaboratively think through solutions to the problems they face in the doing of the DRTA, for that exercise forces students to collaboratively predict and then prove their predictions.

Negotiation is also an integral part of the doing of the cloze as learners discuss possible fillers for the blanks and together decide on appropriate choices. Both techniques integrate students' current world and linguistic knowledge with the information in the text. There are also exercises designed to enlarge students' vocabulary, expand their knowledge of English grammar, and improve their reading and writing skills.

The materials move from simpler to more complex structures, building on what students already know to what they need to learn. Thus, it is advisable to use the book sequentially since there are often references in later lessons to material covered earlier in the book. The directions for the use of the exercises, however, are the same throughout the book. There is always room for you, as the learning facilitator, to use your imagination and creativity to adapt the book to the needs of your particular group of students and institution.

Suggested Procedures: DRTA (Directed Reading and Thinking Activity)

Start this activity by writing the title of the cloze on the board. Then, on the next line, start the sentence, "We're going to find out. . . ." Number the following line with the figure 1. Ask for a student volunteer to write on the board. Tell the students to examine the title carefully and have them use that title to predict everything they think the text (the cloze) will be about or all the information they are going to find in the text. As the students make their predictions collaboratively, the student volunteer writes them on the board. Be sure to "direct" students' examination of the title to features of word order, word endings, meanings, and so on. Try to encourage your students to become very careful observers of the clues in the title so that they will be able to more intelligently guess what the passage will be about. Continue the predicting process for about ten minutes; it will usually be clear to you when to stop. (There are some instances in which students made as many as 60+ predictions; the usual number, however, is about 15–25 predictions.)

Doing the Cloze

Next, divide the class into heterogeneous groups of three. Ask students to read the *entire* passage individually first. Explain that this is what good readers do in order to get a general idea of what the passage is about. This first reading is particularly important in the doing of the cloze, which consists of blanks at regular intervals. Then ask learners to discuss with one another the possibilities for each of the blanks. Explain to students that each filler must be a one-word item that is grammatically correct and semantically appropriate both to the sentence in which it appears as well as to the entire discourse. Encourage students to be sensitive to word endings, punctuation, word order, and clues that appear later on in the passage that can be helpful in the filling of the blanks that appear earlier.

As the class works, you have an opportunity to move from group to group. Watch what students are doing. Listen to their conversations. Observe whether they are paying attention to the clues that are in the text or whether they are simply guessing with little basis in fact. Try to ask questions such as those suggested for the examination of the fillers.

Examining the Fillers

When the class has completed filling the blanks, have students turn their chairs so that they are now sitting in their usual half circle or whatever order your class normally sits in. Now you and your class are ready to start the examination of the fillers, which is a critical step in the use of the cloze for teaching. There are samples of the kinds of questions for you to use in the examination of the fillers for each cloze in the book. They are attached to this section; they are appropriately labeled. You may very well think of additional or other kinds of questions to ask your students as you collaboratively examine the fillers. Similarly, note the kinds of questions that students are asking about reasons for particular choices. Try to give short explanations when you can; postpone lengthier explanations and tell students that you will cover that point at a later date.

Evaluation of Predictions

When all the fillers have been collaboratively examined, go back to the predictions on the board that students made earlier. Direct learners to read each statement and together decide whether the information they had predicted they would find in the text was *explicit, implicit,* or *unknown,* based on their reading. Encourage students to find supporting evidence for their evaluations by going back to the text for specific verification of their opinions. Go through each prediction carefully. Give students ample time to explain the reasons for their choices.

Exercises 5–10

The order in which you do these exercises depends entirely on your needs and preferences and those of your students. You may also decide to do some of these exercises in class and/or at home. Finally, you may want to do some orally, in which case you might not require students to respond in complete sentences as they do in their written work.

TO THE STUDENT

This book is based on my experience with students like you who have come to American colleges or universities to seek a higher education. Because English is your second language, your first goal is to learn to function as an educated, college-level student in your new language.

Therefore, the materials in this book have been designed to use what you already know about your second language and the world to help you learn more about your new language. You will notice that you are continually asked to explain why you are doing particular things or to think about your reasons for making certain choices. The reason for this is simple: Good language learners are aware of what they are doing as they proceed in their learning of a new language. Good language learners guess, ask questions, and think about what they are doing. Good language learners constantly evaluate themselves to find out what they know, what they need to know, and how to get the new knowledge they need. The exercises in this book are designed to help you become a good language learner as you learn to take a more active role in your language learning.

I wish you much success in your adventure with English, and I sincerely hope that these readings and exercises will be of as much benefit to you as they have been to other students of English as a second language.

Unit 1
HOW TO HAVE YOUR HAIR CUT

Exercise 1.
MAKING PREDICTIONS (DRTA)

Directions:

Read the title of the cloze that your teacher has written on the board. Based on the information that you see on the board, see how many predictions you can make about the story that you are about to read.

We are going to complete this sentence:

We're going to find out . . .

Example:

1. We're going to find out why the haircut was special.

Now you and your peers will think of additional predictions as one of your classmates writes them on the board.

_____

_____

_____

_____

_____

_____

_____

_____

_____

_____

_____

_____

_____

_____

_____

_____

Exercise 2.
DOING THE CLOZE

Directions:

Read the entire passage to yourself first. Do not try to fill the blanks before you have completed reading the story. When you have finished reading, you are ready to start working with the other members of your group to fill the blanks. Together, you are going to decide on appropriate fillers for each of the blanks.

There are three rules that you need to remember:

Rule 1. You can use only *one* word to fill the blank.
Rule 2. The word must make sense both to the sentence it is in and to the entire story.
Rule 3. The word you choose must be grammatically correct and spelled correctly.

Note: In the letter to the student, you read that you will need to think about what you are doing. Here is your opportunity to show what you already know about English.

HOW TO HAVE YOUR HAIR CUT

A man enters a _____ with a young boy
(1)
_____ seven or eight years _____ age by the hand.
(2) (3)
_____ man is in a _____ and asks the
(4) (5)
_____ to cut his hair _____ and then the boy's
(6) (7)
_____. The man sits in _____ barber chair, and the
(8) (9)
_____ waits for him. The _____ cuts the man's hair.
(10) (11)
_____ the barber finishes, the _____ gets out of the
(12) (13)
_____ and seats the boy _____ the chair. He then
(14) (15)
_____ himself and repeats that _____ is in a great
(16) (17)
_____. The man tells the _____ to go ahead and
(18) (19)
_____ the boy's hair and that _____ will be back in
(20) (21)
_____ few minutes to pay _____ them
(22) (23)
both. He leaves, _____ the barber goes on _____
(24) (25)
cut the boy's hair. _____ barber finishes cutting the
(26)
_____ hair, picks the boy _____, and seats him in
(27) (28)
_____ chair at the side _____ wait. A half hour
(29) (30)
_____. An hour passes. The _____ says to the child:
(31) (32)
" _____ worry. Your father will _____ back soon."
(33) (34)
"My father? _____ he isn't my father,"
(35)
_____ boy protests. "I was _____ in the street when
(36) (37)
_____ came along and said: ' _____ on with me, little
(38) (39)
_____. Let's go in this _____ together and have our
(40) (41)
_____ cut!' "
(42)

Exercise 3.
EXAMINING THE FILLERS FOR THE CLOZE

Directions:

Look at the choices you have made for the blanks in your text as each person reads a sentence with the fillers he or she has chosen for the blanks. If your choice differs from the one you hear, and you are not sure if your answer is correct, ask your teacher to explain. Often there is more than one appropriate filler for the blank. Check to see whether you have spelled the word correctly and whether you have put the capital letters, periods, and other punctuation marks where they belong.

Exercise 4.
EXAMINATION OF PREDICTIONS

Directions:

As you and your class go over each prediction that you made earlier, you are going to decide whether the statement is *implicit, explicit,* or *unknown,* based on the story you have just read. Be sure to ask your teacher if these words are not clear to you. As you read each prediction, think about what you have read in the story and then decide. It will often be necessary to go back to the text and find justification for your answer.

Exercise 5.
READER RESPONSE SHEET

Directions:

Please answer the following questions in complete sentences.

Example:

1. Why do you think the author wrote the story?
   The author wrote the story to entertain the reader.

Or: _____

2. Do you think she or he was successful in achieving the aim? Why? Why not?

_____

3. What are some questions that you have about the story?

Example:

Why was the man in such a hurry?

_____

_____

_____

_____

_____

_____

_____

_____

4. What are some words or expressions that are not clear to you?

_____   _____   _____

_____   _____   _____

5. What two things did you find out from doing the cloze, and how are you going to practice them? Please be specific.

_____

_____

_____

_____

_____

_____

_____

_____

Exercise 6.
COMPREHENSION/DISCUSSION QUESTIONS

Directions:

Please read the following questions. Discuss them with your peers, and then write the answers in complete sentences.

Example:

1. How would you describe the man in the story?
   The man in the story seemed to be strange.

2. What kind of person do you think the barber is?

   _____

   _____

3. Is the barber the kind of person you'd like to do business with? Why?
   Why not?

   _____

   _____

4. How would you like to do business with the man who came for a
   haircut?

   _____

   _____

5. What do you think of the little boy?

   _____

   _____

6. Do you think it was wise of the little boy to go with the man? Why?
   Why not?

   _____

   _____

7. Do children in your country play unsupervised in the street?

   _____

8. If you had or have a child, would you allow your child to play on the
   street in New York? Why? Why not?

   _____

   _____

9. If you were the barber, how would you feel when the little boy told you the man was not his father? Did something like that ever happen to you? What did you do about it?

_____

_____

_____

_____

Exercise 7.
GRAMMAR POINT

Simple Present

The simple present tense in English is known as the timeless, factual, general, or habitual tense. Some examples, which follow, will make each of these meanings of the simple present tense clearer to you. Since you have been studying English for some time now, these meanings of the simple present tense may be somewhat familiar to you.

Form:

The simple present tense is formed by using the base form of the verb for all persons, singular and plural, *except for* the third person singular, as follows:

I, we	leave
you (singular), you (plural)	leave
they	leave
he, she, it	leave*s*

A. The simple present tense is timeless because it expresses happenings that are not tied to any specific time but rather carry the important connotation of regularity.

Examples:

I go to school.

He showers every morning.

They buy Christmas presents every year.

We have a leap year every four years.

Directions:

Write a paragraph in which you tell about some things that happen regularly or all the time. Try to use time expressions like *every three minutes, once a week, twice a year,* and so on.

_____

_____

_____

_____

_____

_____

_____

B. Another use of the simple present tense is to talk about natural or scientific phenomena.

Examples:

Water freezes at 32°F.

The sun rises in the east.

The stars shine at night.

Directions:

Write a paragraph in which you use the simple present tense to describe some scientific or natural phenomena.

_____

_____

_____

_____

_____

_____

_____

C. A third use of the simple present tense is to express feelings or opinions.

Examples:

I like you.

I think learning a new language is fun.

Directions:

What examples can *you* think of?

_____

_____

_____

_____

_____

_____

D. A fourth common use of the simple present tense is to indicate the future with particular verbs. The following verbs are often used in the simple present; we need to remember that they mean future.

open/close   *begin/end*   *arrive/leave*   *land/depart*

Directions:

Write three sentences with the words in italics. Be sure you mean future.

Examples:

The train leaves at 10 tomorrow.

School closes on Friday.

_____

_____

_____

_____

_____

It is possible to include all four meanings of the simple present tense in one paragraph.

Example:
In the wintertime, it gets dark early. Therefore, I prefer to register for morning classes. In that way, I go to school and come home in daylight. School opens next week.

Do you see how all four meanings of the simple present tense were expressed in the paragraph? Which meaning of the simple present tense did you find in the first sentence? in the second? in the third? in the fourth? Write those meanings on the following lines.

sentence 1 _____

sentence 2 _____

sentence 3 _____

sentence 4 _____

Directions:
Write a paragraph in which you describe some of your activities. Try to include each of the four meanings of the simple present tense. Review those meanings as they appear in the earlier section of this exercise.

_____

_____

_____

_____

_____

_____

_____

Reread the story "How to Have Your Hair Cut." Find all the verbs used in the simple present tense. Do they fit the meanings that you just learned for that tense or is there an additional meaning for the simple present tense that we did not yet talk about?

Yes, you are right. There is an additional meaning of this tense. That meaning is called the "historical present" and it is often used in the telling of stories such as the one we just read. Sometimes we use the historical present to report on something we have read or to tell a joke. Read the following:

A man comes home from work. He is very hungry. He says to his wife, "Is dinner ready yet?"
"No," she answers.
"I'm hungry. I think I'll go out to eat."
"Wait ten minutes," says his wife.
"Why? Will dinner be ready then?"
"No," answers his wife, "but I'll be ready to go with you."

The simple present tense was used in this dialogue to indicate what we call the "historical present." It is also used to talk about what we read.

Example:

In the newspaper, the journalist says that prices are going down.

Directions:

Write a paragraph or a short story that you might tell a friend. See whether you can make it funny. Use as many meanings of the simple present tense as you can. Refer back to the information above to guide you.

_____

_____

_____

_____

_____

_____

_____

_____

_____

_____

_____

_____

_____

_____

_____

Exercise 8.
WORD BUILDING

Compounds

In English, we form new words in many ways; these methods of making new words enrich the English vocabulary and make it possible for speakers of English to express themselves more accurately.

A. One way to make new words is to take two nouns and combine them to form one new word. We call this new word a "compound word," and this word often includes the meanings of both parts. For example, we read about a visit to a *barbershop*. What are the two words in *barbershop*?

_____   _____

What do we call these kinds of words? _____

How do you know? _____

This kind of compound word is treated like any other noun in English.
To form the plural we add *s:* barbershop – barbershop*s*
To show possession, we add *'s:*

The barbershop*'s* owner was a kind man.

Here are some other, similar words:

bookstore   classroom   bedroom   newspaper   paintbrush

Can you think of any words that fit this category?

_____   _____   _____

B. Another way of making compound words is to combine a noun with a verb. In the story we read about a *haircut*. This word is made up of the noun *hair* and the verb *cut*. There are many examples of this kind of combining in English. Here are some:

headache   sunshine   crybaby   nightfall   sunset

Can you think of any words that fit this category?

——————————   ——————————   ——————————

C. Other compound words are made up of prepositions and nouns, verbs, or adjectives. Here are some examples of these compound words:

preposition + noun: outlaw

preposition + verb: bypass

preposition + adjective: overripe

Are all of these compound words nouns? ——————————————

Why? Why not? ——————————————————————

——————————————————————————————

Summary:

Each of the following combinations is called a compound word.

noun + noun: windowpane

noun + verb: sunshine

preposition + noun: outlaw

preposition + verb: bypass

These words are used as nouns, verbs, or adjectives. They follow the regular pattern of use for these kinds of words in English. We have already talked about the noun. Now let's look at the word *bypass*. It can be used as a verb.

Example:

The highway *bypasses* the heavy city traffic.

Recently, the word *bypass* has also been used as a noun to describe a particular kind of heart surgery. Thus, we can say: He had a *bypass*. Or: He had a *bypass* operation. Is the word *bypass* a noun, a verb, or an adjective in these sentences?

——————————————————————————————

——————————————————————————————

——————————————————————————————

Note: Sometimes it is easy to figure out the meaning of the compound word by looking at each of its parts. In other cases, the meaning of the compound word is not truly related to each of the parts. Here are some examples:

hothead   rainbow   offspring   shortcoming

In these cases, we need to know the exact meaning of the word. When you are not sure what the word means after you have examined all the context clues, use a dictionary. Can you think of some compound words that have not been mentioned?

_____   _____   _____

_____   _____   _____

Directions:

Write a paragraph about something scientific or something that happens in nature. See how many compound words you can use. Remember to use the simple present tense where appropriate. You might start like this:

The sunset is usually beautiful to watch.

_____

_____

_____

_____

_____

_____

_____

_____

Exercise 9.
WRITING ACTIVITIES

Directions:

Please read the following suggested topics. Then choose one topic and write about it.

1. Rewrite the story in your own words. You may write it either exactly as it happened or use your own imagination to create a new story. You might pretend that you are telling a friend about the story that you read in class today.

2. In groups of three, write a dialogue in which you describe an imaginary conversation between a man in a hurry and a child. Remember that

the child, like all children, is not really anxious to have his or her hair cut. In your dialogue, show how the man persuades the child to accompany him to the barbershop. One of you will be the narrator.

3. Write about something that someone forced you to do. What were you forced to do? How did you feel about it? For example, you might like to write about your coming to the United States. Did you come here because someone forced you to do so, or did you come here of your own free will? Or, you may be attending college because that is what your parents want you to do. If that is true, write about it. Try to give as many details as you can so that your reader will be able to appreciate your situation.

4. It is clear that the man played a trick on the barber. How do you think the barber feels? How would you feel if you were the barber?

Has anybody ever played a trick on you? Please write about it. In your writing, include the people involved and describe what happened, how you felt, and what you did. How do you feel now about how you reacted then? Would you react differently at this moment?

5. Please choose your own topic to write about.

Exercise 10.
DICTATION

Directions:

Your teacher will dictate the following sentences to you. Your job is to write them as accurately as you can. As you write your sentences, remember to use correct spelling and punctuation. Finally, even if you don't hear every word clearly, try to use all the clues in the sentence to help you figure out the difficult word. Do what you have practiced in the doing of the cloze.

1. A man and a little boy enter a barbershop.
2. The man is in a very big hurry.
3. He tells the barber to cut his hair and leaves.
4. He promises to come back to pay.
5. Then the barber gives the boy a haircut.
6. After his haircut, the boy waits for the man.
7. Time passes, but the man does not return.
8. The kind barber tells the little boy not to worry.
9. He says that his father will be back soon.
10. The surprised boy says the man is not his father.

Unit 2
PEOPLE'S BEST FRIEND

Exercise 1.
MAKING PREDICTIONS (DRTA)

Directions:

Read the title of the cloze that your teacher has written on the board. Based on the information that you see on the board, see how many predictions you can make about the story that you are about to read.

We are going to complete this sentence:

We're going to find out . . .

Example:

1. We're going to find out who people's best friend is.

Now you and your peers will think of additional predictions as one of your classmates writes them on the board.

_____

_____

_____

_____

_____

_____

_____

_____

_____

_____

_____

_____

_____

_____

_____

_____

_____

Exercise 2.
DOING THE CLOZE

Directions:

Read the entire passage to yourself first. Do not try to fill the blanks before you have completed reading the story. When you have finished reading, you are ready to start working with the other members of your group to fill the blanks. Together, you are going to decide on appropriate fillers for each of the blanks.

There are three rules that you need to remember:

Rule 1.   You can use only *one* word to fill the blank.
Rule 2.   The word must make sense both to the sentence it is in and to the entire story.
Rule 3.   The word you choose must be grammatically correct and spelled correctly.

Note: In the letter to the student, you read that you will need to think about what you are doing. Here is your opportunity to show what you already know about English.

PEOPLE'S BEST FRIEND

Almost everyone likes dogs, ___(1)___ almost everyone likes to ___(2)___ stories about dogs. Here ___(3)___ a short story about ___(4)___ Seeing Eye dog. A ___(5)___ Eye dog is a ___(6)___ dog that helps blind ___(7)___ walk along the streets ___(8)___ do many other things. ___(9)___ call them "Seeing Eye" ___(10)___ because these dogs are ___(11)___ "eyes" of the blind ___(12)___ and they help them ___(13)___ "see."

These dogs generally ___(14)___ to special schools for ___(15)___ months to learn how ___(16)___ help blind people.

One ___(17)___ a Seeing Eye dog ___(18)___ an old, blind man ___(19)___ on a bus together. ___(20)___ bus was full of ___(21)___, and there were no ___(22)___. One man, however, soon ___(23)___ up and left his ___(24)___. The dog led the ___(25)___ man to the seat, ___(26)___ there was very little ___(27)___. The dog started to ___(28)___ the people on each ___(29)___ gently with its nose. ___(30)___ pushed and pushed until ___(31)___ people moved over, and ___(32)___ there was enough space ___(33)___ two people. Then the ___(34)___ man sat down and ___(35)___ dog got up on ___(36)___ seat at the side ___(37)___ the blind man. He ___(38)___ down on the seat ___(39)___ put his head on ___(40)___ leg of the blind ___(41)___. He was very comfortable ___(42)___ soon fell asleep.

Everyone ___(43)___ the bus had to ___(44)___ at the cleverness of ___(45)___ dog in making space ___(46)___ the blind man and ___(47)___ the same time making ___(48)___ place for himself. When ___(49)___ was time to get ___(50)___ the bus, the dog ___(51)___ up and led his ___(52)___ to the door (exit).

Exercise 3.
EXAMINING THE FILLERS FOR THE CLOZE

Directions:

Look at the choices you have made for the blanks in your text as each person reads a sentence with the fillers he or she has chosen for the blanks. If your choice differs from the one you hear, and you are not sure if your answer is correct, ask your teacher to explain. Often there is more than one appropriate filler for the blank. Check to see whether you have spelled the word correctly and whether you have put the capital letters, periods, and other punctuation marks where they belong.

Exercise 4.
EXAMINATION OF PREDICTIONS

Directions:

As you and your class go over each prediction that you made earlier, you are going to decide whether the statement is *implicit, explicit,* or *unknown,* based on the story you have just read. Be sure to ask your teacher if these words are not clear to you. As you read each prediction, think about what you have read in the story and then decide. It will often be necessary to go back to the text and find justification for your answer.

Exercise 5.
READER RESPONSE SHEET

Directions:

Please answer the following questions in complete sentences.

Example:

1. What kind of dog is this story about?
   This story is about a Seeing Eye dog.

Or: _____

2. Do you think the story took place in a city or in a small village? Why?

_____

_____

_____

_____

3. Who uses the services of a Seeing Eye dog?

_____

_____

_____

_____

4. Do Seeing Eye dogs need special training? Why? Why not?

_____

_____

_____

_____

5. What questions do you have about the story?

Example:

Why didn't people get up and give the blind man a seat?

_____

_____

_____

_____

_____

_____

_____

_____

_____

_____

_____

6. What are some words or expressions that are not clear to you?

_____   _____   _____

_____   _____   _____

7. What two things did you learn from doing this cloze? Please be specific.

_____

_____

_____

_____

_____

_____

_____

_____

_____

Exercise 6.
COMPREHENSION/DISCUSSION QUESTIONS

Directions:

Please read the following questions. Discuss them with your peers, and then write the answers in complete sentences.

Example:

1. How would you describe the passengers on the bus?
   The passengers on the bus were selfish and inconsiderate.

2. Why do you think it is necessary for Seeing Eye dogs to have special training?

_____

_____

_____

3. Why do you think this story took place in a city and not in a small town?

_____

_____

_____

_____

4. How do you think you would feel if you had to use a Seeing Eye dog?

_____

_____

_____

_____

5. How do people in your country react to others who are handicapped?

_____

_____

_____

_____

_____

_____

_____

6. If you were in charge of a city, would you make special arrangements
   for handicapped people? Why? Why not?

_____

_____

_____

_____

_____

_____

_____

7. If you had been on that bus, would you have given your seat to the old, blind man? Why? Why not?

_____

_____

_____

_____

_____

_____

_____

_____

Exercise 7.
GRAMMAR POINT

Simple Past

The simple past tense in English is used to denote an action that began and was completed in the past. We often use a definite time expression to denote that action. We say: I watched TV last night. I went shopping last week. Thus, it makes no difference whether that past action is recent, five minutes ago, or more distant, five years ago.

We also often use the word *ago* in past tense sentences.

Examples:

I saw a Seeing Eye dog three weeks ago.

I came to New York two years ago.

Form:

The past tense in English is usually formed by adding *ed* to the base form of the verb.

Example:

walk + *ed* = walked

There is no change in the ending for any of the speakers, so we use the verb *walked* in the same way for all speakers:

I walked   we walked
you (singular) walked   you (plural) walked
he, she, it walked   they walked

In addition, even though we add *ed* to many verbs in English, there are differences in the way that *ed* is pronounced.

In words ending in the *sound d* or *t,* the *ed* ending is pronounced as an additional syllable. Therefore, *needed* is pronounced *need + ed.* That second syllable, or part of the word, is pronounced with the *i* sound found in the word *it.*

The word *rent,* ending with the *t* sound, is pronounced *rent + ed.*

Similarly, *decide* becomes *decided,* and we pronounce it as a *two-syllable,* or *two-part, word.* Why is this so? You remember that we said earlier that the rule applies to the last *sound* of the word, not the last *letter.*

There is another pronunciation rule for words ending in *voiced* and *unvoiced sounds.* When we pronounce a *voiced sound,* we can feel the vibrations if we put our fingers on our throat as we say it, as in the word *love* or *save. Love* and *save* become *loved* and *saved* with a *d* sound at the end.

However, we don't feel the vibrations of an *unvoiced sound* when we put our fingers on our throat. The word *walk,* ending in an *unvoiced sound,* becomes *walked;* we pronounce it with a *t* sound in the past.

To form the *negative* in the past, we use the word *did + not +* the *base form* of the verb. Thus, we say:

The dog *did not forget* to find a seat for his master.
    didn't

The dog *did not leave* his master alone; he sat next to him.
    didn't

The verb *to be* forms the past differently just as we saw when we studied the simple present in the last unit.

Example:

The dog *was* intelligent.
The man and his dog *were* finally comfortable.

The forms of the verb *to be* in the past are as follows:

I was	we were
you (singular) were	you (plural) were
he, she, it was	they were

We said that the *ed* ending is usually used to show the simple past tense in English. But there are many English verbs that do not follow this pattern. At the back of this book, in the Appendix, you will find a list of the most common irregular past tense verbs in English. There is no easy way to help you learn these forms. YOU SIMPLY MUST MEMORIZE THEM. As you have probably realized by now, memorizing is a useful language-learning strategy. Memorizing the irregular past tense verbs is a good example of the importance of memorizing in the process of learning a new language. That's the bad news. The good news is that once you have learned the irregular verbs, you don't have to learn them again.

Directions:

Write a paragraph in which you tell about things that started and were completed in the past. You might start your paragraph in the following way:

Three weeks ago I was on the bus on my way to school. I saw a handicapped woman get on the bus. Nobody got up to give the woman a seat. That surprised me. I expected Americans to be polite.

Now write your own paragraph. See how many irregular verbs from the Appendix you can include in your writing. Many of these irregular verbs are used by speakers of English all the time.

_____

_____

_____

_____

_____

_____

_____

Exercise 8.
WORD BUILDING

Word Forms

There were two main characters in the story we just read — an old, blind man and a Seeing Eye dog. We read how the blind man depended on the dog to direct him and warn him of danger.

We read about the *blindness* of the old man and the *cleverness* of the dog. The story also described the *dependence* of the blind man on the dog.

In English, we change the root form of the word as we use it to perform a variety of functions.

For example, we can talk about the describing function of the word and use the adjective form — *blind*. The *blind* man got on the bus.

the verb form – *to become blind*   The old man *became blind.*
the noun form – *the blindness*   The *blindness* of the old man
                                       made him dependent on others for
                                       assistance.
the adverb form – *blindly**   He followed the instructions
                                       blindly.

Thus, in modern English, the function of the word in the sentence often determines its form. As students of English as a second language, we need to be aware of the various forms to help us understand what we read and to increase our ability to express ourselves in our new language.

Here are some sentences using the root word *to smile* in a variety of ways:

The passengers *smiled* at the cleverness of the dog. (verb)

The *smiling* passengers petted the dog. (adjective)

There was a *smile* on the face of all the passengers. (noun)

---

*This meaning is slightly different from that of sightlessness. To follow somebody blindly means to do what somebody else says without question. (You can easily see how this additional meaning came from the root word referring to no sight.)

Here are some groups of words that belong to the same family. See whether you can fit them into the appropriate blanks.

> to train
> a trainer
> a training period
> the training
> trained

Seeing Eye dogs need to be specially _____. The _____ of these dogs requires both a competent _____ and a _____ period of several months. Then the _____ dog is ready to serve the needs of the blind person.

> to differentiate (or to make a difference)
> the difference
> different
> differently

It is usually quite simple to _____ a handicapped person. Handicapped people look _____ from other people. Because of their handicap, they often behave _____ from others. However, a physical _____ does not mean that the handicapped person is a _____ human being from the rest of us. _____ does not mean deficient.

> to be interested in
> an interest
> interesting
> interested
> interestingly

When we think of _____ people, we think of those that everybody _____ _____ _____. An _____ person is one who takes an _____ in many different things. Such people live their lives _____, and they are _____ to the rest of us.

Now you think of some families of words that are not yet clear to you (or perhaps are giving you trouble). What are they?

_____   _____   _____

_____   _____   _____

How will you try to find out the forms of the words you need? Yes, you might ask your teacher. Where else do you think you might find such information? Yes, a dictionary contains that kind of information too.

Directions:

Write your own paragraph, using some word forms that are now clearer to you. We will do more work on word forms in the next unit.

Your paragraph might start something like the following:

I was interested in the story about the Seeing Eye dog because many more handicapped people are visible nowadays. I greatly admire people who are determined to overcome their handicaps. They are often courageous, interesting people and knowing them can prove to be a rewarding experience for us.

_____

_____

_____

_____

_____

_____

_____

_____

Exercise 9.
WRITING ACTIVITIES

Directions:

Please read the following suggested topics. Then choose one topic and write about it.

1. Rewrite the story in your own words. You might like to write about your observation of that bus ride and your reaction to the behavior of the Americans.

2. Choose a partner and write a dialogue describing a blind person coming to a school for Seeing Eye dogs to choose such a dog for him- or herself. **Or:** Write a dialogue describing the conversation of two people on the bus who are talking to each other about the event of the dog and the blind man.

3. Just as there are special training schools for animals, there are, as you know, special training schools for human beings. Some people go to special schools to learn how to work with airplanes, while others specialize in keeping all kinds of complicated records. Tell what you know about two such schools in your country and show, if you can, how they are the same or different from training schools in the United States.

4. Handicapped people are more visible nowadays because there is a greater awareness of their need for special facilities. Many public buildings now have ramps and/or elevators for easy access by the handicapped. Public buses are specially built to accommodate the handicapped. This is as it should be. In a democratic society everybody should have access to public facilities. People with special needs should be able to lead lives that are as normal as possible.

Do you agree or disagree?

Write an essay the very best way you can. Use your knowledge of the world, what you have read and/or what you have studied to support your opinion.

5. Please choose your own topic and write about it.

Exercise 10.
DICTATION

Directions:

Your teacher will dictate the following sentences to you. Your job is to write them as accurately as you can. As you write your sentences, remember to use correct spelling and punctuation. Finally, even if you don't hear every word clearly, try to use all the clues in the sentence to help you figure out the difficult word. Do what you have practiced in the doing of the cloze.

1. A blind man and a Seeing Eye dog got on a bus together.
2. The bus was full of people.
3. There was no seat for the old, blind man.
4. Soon a man got up and left his seat.
5. The dog led his master to the empty seat.
6. However, there was not enough room for the dog.
7. With his nose, the Seeing Eye dog made the people move over.
8. Then he got up on the seat next to his master.
9. The people smiled at the intelligence of the dog.
10. The dog led the blind man to the exit.

Unit 3
THE OBSERVANT STUDENTS
AND THEIR CLEVER PROFESSOR

Exercise 1.
MAKING PREDICTIONS (DRTA)

Directions:

Read the title of the cloze that your teacher has written on the board. Based on the information that you see on the board, see how many predictions you can make about the story that you are about to read.

We are going to complete this sentence:

We're going to find out . . .

Example:

1. We're going to find out what the students observed.

Now you and your peers will think of additional predictions as one of your classmates writes them on the board.

_____

_____

_____

_____

_____

_____

_____

_____

_____

_____

_____

_____

_____

_____

_____

_____

Exercise 2.
DOING THE CLOZE

Directions:

Read the entire passage to yourself first. Do not try to fill the blanks before you have completed reading the story. When you have finished reading, you are ready to start working with the other members of your group to fill the blanks. Together, you are going to decide on appropriate fillers for each of the blanks.

There are three rules that you need to remember:

Rule 1. You can use only *one* word to fill the blank.
Rule 2. The word must make sense both to the sentence it is in and to the entire story.
Rule 3. The word you choose must be grammatically correct and spelled correctly.

Note: In the letter to the student, you read that you will need to think about what you are doing. Here is your opportunity to show what you already know about English.

THE OBSERVANT STUDENTS AND THEIR CLEVER PROFESSOR

Professor Jones did not _____ (1) to have long hair. _____ (2) he used to forget _____ (3) there were barbers in _____ (4) world until somebody reminded _____ (5). Then he used to _____ (6) and have his hair _____ (7) quite short. This meant _____ (8) sometimes he went around _____ (9) long hair for several _____ (10), or even several months, _____ (11) then suddenly came to _____ (12) of his lectures with _____ (13) short hair.

After some _____ (14), his students began to _____ (15) on the date of _____ (16) next visit to the _____ (17). Whenever his hair became _____ (18) enough to need cutting, _____ (19) jar and a piece _____ (20) paper were put on _____ (21) table outside the professor's _____ (22). Students who wanted to _____ (23) used to put a _____ (24) into the jar and _____ (25) their name and the _____ (26) they had chosen on _____ (27) piece of paper. The _____ (28) who correctly guessed the _____ (29) of the professor's next _____ (30) to the barber won _____ (31) the money in the _____ (32).

Professor Jones was very _____ (33) by the jar and _____ (34) that appeared on the _____ (35) one day, stayed there _____ (36) several weeks, then disappeared _____ (37) quite a long time, _____ (38) then appeared again.

But _____ (39) was a clever man _____ (40) a university professor of _____ (41), so he began to _____ (42) down the dates on _____ (43) the jar and the _____ (44) appeared and disappeared and _____ (45) study them carefully. After _____ (46) few months, he suddenly _____ (47)

what they meant. When _____ finished his next lecture,
(48)

_____ stopped at the table, _____ a dollar into the
(49)   (50)

_____, wrote his name and _____ day's date on the
(51)   (52)

_____, went to the barber, _____ then came back to
(53)   (54)

_____ the jar of money _____ he had won.
(55)   (56)

Exercise 3.
EXAMINING THE FILLERS FOR THE CLOZE

Directions:

Look at the choices you have made for the blanks in your text as each person reads a sentence with the fillers he or she has chosen for the blanks. If your choice differs from the one you hear, and you are not sure if your answer is correct, ask your teacher to explain. Often there is more than one appropriate filler for the blank. Check to see whether you have spelled the word correctly and whether you have put the capital letters, periods, and other punctuation marks where they belong.

Exercise 4.
EXAMINATION OF PREDICTIONS

Directions:

As you and your class go over each prediction that you had made earlier, you are going to decide whether the statement is *implicit, explicit,* or *unknown,* based on the story you have just read. Be sure to ask your teacher if these words are not clear to you. As you read each prediction, think about what you have read in the story and then decide. It will often be necessary to go back to the text and find justification for your answer.

Exercise 5.
READER RESPONSE SHEET

Directions:

Please answer the following questions in complete sentences.

Example:

1. Why do you think the author wrote this story?
   The author wrote this story to give readers an enjoyable reading experience.

2. Do you think the author achieved his or her aim? Why? Why not?

_____

_____

_____

_____

3. Who do you think thought of the idea of a bet? Why?

_____

_____

_____

4. What are some questions that you have about the story?

Example:

Why were the students so interested in the professor's hair?

_____

_____

_____

_____

_____

_____

_____

5. Do you think you and your peers would be interested in such a bet? Why? Why not?

_____

_____

_____

_____

6. What are some words and/or expressions that are still not clear to you?

_____ _____ _____

_____ _____ _____

7. What two things did you learn from doing this cloze, and how are you
    going to practice them? Please be specific.

_____

_____

_____

_____

_____

_____

Exercise 6.
COMPREHENSION/DISCUSSION QUESTIONS

Directions:

Please read the following questions. Discuss them with your peers, and
then write the answers in complete sentences.

Example:

1. What words would you use to describe the professor?
    The professor was forgetful, curious, etc. What else?

_____

_____

_____

2. Why do you think the students cared about the professor's hair? Do
    you think you and your colleagues would be similarly concerned
    about the appearance of your professor?

_____

_____

_____

_____

3. What kind of university do you imagine that this story took place in?
    Why?

_____

_____

_____

4. What do you think of the betting method the students chose?

_____

_____

_____

_____

_____

5. How do you think this story supports the popular view that professors are absentminded? We call an image of this kind, generally held by many people, a "stereotype." For example, when we ride in the subway, we often imagine what kind of people our fellow passengers are without really knowing them. We make these guesses or have these images of people on the basis of our own stereotypes.

_____

_____

_____

_____

_____

_____

_____

6. What do you think of the phenomenon of stereotyping? Can you think of any situation in which stereotyping might be helpful? Please explain.

_____

_____

_____

_____

_____

_____

_____

7. It is true that people are often judged by their appearance. What significance do some people attach to long hair on men? Is this the same or different from the view of men with long hair generally held in your country?

_____

_____

_____

_____

_____

_____

8. Professor Jones obviously had a good sense of humor and immediately entered into the betting game with his students. How do you think a professor in your country would have responded in a similar kind of situation?

_____

_____

_____

_____

_____

_____

9. How do you think the students reacted when they discovered what the professor had done? How would you have reacted if you had been one of those students?

_____

_____

_____

_____

_____

_____

Exercise 7.
GRAMMAR POINT

Past Perfect

In Unit 2, we learned that we use the simple past tense when we want to talk about something that started and was completed in the past. Sometimes we need to talk about more than one occurrence that took place in the past. If both or all those actions took place at the same time, we could still use the simple past for each action.

Example:

> This morning I got up at 6:30. I showered, got dressed, ate breakfast, and went to school.

However, there are times when two actions that occur in the past do not take place at the same time. That is, one action takes place before the other. In that case, we need to be able to indicate that fact in our grammar so that the listener or reader can easily recognize not only what happened but when it happened. We use the *past perfect* to mark that action that took place *before* another action although both were started and completed in the past.

Example:

> The professor noticed that the students had put the jar and the piece of paper on the table.

The two actions that occurred in the above sentence are

The professor noticed something.
The students put something on the table.

Which came first? You're right. There had to be something on the table for the professor to notice. Therefore, what the students did preceded the professor's noticing, and we need to use the past perfect to indicate that action.

Form:

The past perfect is formed by the helping (auxiliary) verb *had + past participle*. Please remember that *had* is a helping verb and *never* changes its form. So we say:

> I, we
> you (singular), you (plural)   had
> he, she, it
> they

Similarly, the past participle form of the verb remains the same and *never* changes regardless of the subject.

Thus, we say: I had put. We had put. You had put, etc.

We can also call the past participle the *d-t-n* form of the verb. The final *sound* of the past participle form determines what category it belongs in. For example:

> save – saved   walk – walked   write — written
> d   t   n

In addition, as we learned in Unit 2, in words ending in the *d* or *t* sound, we add another syllable so that *decide* is

> pronounced decid*ed,*   need becomes need*ed,*   rent becomes rent*ed.*
> id   id   id

That additional syllable is prounced as the *i* in *it + d.*

Here are some examples of sentences with the past perfect:

1. They never received the furniture they had ordered.
2. He realized that the students had played a trick on him.
3. They asked the immigrants why they had come to the United States.

Moreover, since the purpose of the past perfect is to indicate one action in the past which precedes another, it is not necessary to use the past perfect in sentences that contain the words *before* or *after,* which are, after all, time markers themselves. Therefore, the past perfect is often omitted in sentences that include these words. This is particularly true

when we speak; when we write, we may wish to be more formal.
Thus, we say:

They ate breakfast before they left home.

instead of the more formal sentence:

They had eaten breakfast before they left home.

Directions:

Write a paragraph in which you describe some events that occurred before others. For example, you might write about your plans for life in the United States before you actually came here. Your first sentence might be this:

> **I had thought I would learn English quickly when I was in my country.**
>
> Or: **The meeting took longer than we had planned.**
>
> Or: **Professor Jones had forgotten that there were barbers in the world. His hair grew very long because he had forgotten to take a haircut. His students had made a plan and they bet on the date of the haircut.**

Now you write your paragraph:

_____

_____

_____

_____

_____

_____

_____

_____

_____

Exercise 8.
WORD BUILDING

Past Participles, Adjectives

In English, we often use the verb *to be* + *the past participle* as idioms to indicate special meanings. Thus, although we often use this structure to indicate the passive, we can use it to indicate special meanings, as we shall see below.

For example, we can say:

I am determined to learn English.

Or: I am scared to speak English.

These are special uses of the passive.

The following are some verbs that are used in this special way. They are formed by *to be* + *past participle:*

to be used to

to be accustomed to

to be divorced from

to be engaged in

to be married to

to be interested in

to be opposed to

to be scared to

to be disappointed in

to be worried about

to be supposed to

There are several things we need to note about this way of adding to our vocabulary.

1. The time is indicated by the verb *to be;* as we said earlier, the past participle *never* changes. For example:

The students are interested in their professor's hair.

The students were interested in betting on the date for the haircut.

The professor will also be interested in the bet.

2. This is an idiomatic use of the structure, and although it looks like the passive, it isn't. There is no agent or doer of the action. The meaning expressed has no connection with the passive.

3. There is often a little word or preposition that follows the past participle. There are few of these idiomatic expressions to remember; memorizing them should be something you can easily do.

In addition, we can change the position of the past participles and make them into modifiers or adjectives, so we can say

The students *were determined* to bet on the date of the professor's haircut.

What kind of students were they? They were *determined* students.

The professor *is interested* in the bet.

What kind of professor is he? He is an *interested* professor.

By using the past participle before the noun, we can increase our vocabulary and use words that we know in different ways to create new meanings.

Directions:

Look at the list of past participles on page 46. Think of some sentences or a paragraph that you might write using the past participle as an adjective. Your paragraph might look like this:

The *determined* students set out to play a joke on the professor. However, the *interested* professor soon discovered their trick. There were some *disappointed* students in the class when they discovered what the professor had done.

Now write your paragraph.

_____

_____

_____

_____

_____

_____

_____

_____

_____

_____

Exercise 9.
WRITING ACTIVITIES

Directions:

Please read the following suggested topics. Then choose one topic and write about it.

1. Rewrite the story in your own words. You may rewrite it from the students' point of view. For example, you might start your rewrite the following way:

When I was a student at _____ University, we were very interested in the length of our absentminded professor's hair.

2. In groups of 3 or 4, write a dialogue that could have taken place between the professor and several of his students. Try to make it funny if you can. Or you might write a dialogue that took place among the students as they planned their strategy for fooling the professor.

3. There are often times when we feel we would like to bet on something. We seem to feel very certain one way or the other, and we feel

compelled to prove that we were right.

Please write about such an occasion in your life. Be sure to include all the details so that you answer the questions *who, what, when, where, why,* and *how.*

4. The students in the professor's class were interested in trivia. Students who spend time thinking about the length of their professor's hair indicate that they are not serious about their studies. Such students will probably never become competent professionals.

Do you agree or disagree?

Write an essay the very best way you can. Use your knowledge of the world, what you have read, and/or what you have studied to support your point of view.

5. Please choose your own topic to write about.

Exercise 10.
DICTATION

Directions:

Your teacher will dictate the following sentences to you. Your job is to write them as accurately as you can. As you write your sentences, remember to correct spelling and punctuation. Finally, even if you don't hear every word clearly, try to use all the clues in the sentence to help you figure out the difficult word. Do what you have practiced in the doing of the cloze.

1. The professor wasn't opposed to a haircut.
2. But he had forgotten to have his hair cut.
3. His students were interested in their professor's hair.
4. They noticed when he had taken a haircut.
5. They were accustomed to the professor's long hair.
6. He saw they had put a jar on the table.
7. The students were supposed to guess the date.
8. They wrote the date on a piece of paper.
9. Professor Jones was very interested in the paper and the jar.
10. The students were disappointed in the bet.

Unit 4
AN UNDISCIPLINED SOLDIER

Exercise 1.
MAKING PREDICTIONS (DRTA)

Directions:

Read the title of the cloze that your teacher has written on the board. Based on the information that you see on the board, see how many predictions you can make about the story that you are about to read.

We are going to complete this sentence:

We're going to find out . . .

Example:

1. We're going to find out why the soldier was undisciplined.

Now you and your peers will think of additional predictions as one of your classmates writes them on the board.

_____

_____

_____

_____

_____

_____

_____

_____

_____

_____

_____

_____

_____

_____

_____

Exercise 2.
DOING THE CLOZE

Directions:

Read the entire passage to yourself first. Do not try to fill the blanks before you have completed reading the story. When you have finished reading, you are ready to start working with the other members of your group to fill the blanks. Together, you are going to decide on appropriate fillers for each of the blanks.

There are three rules that you need to remember:

Rule 1. You can use only *one* word to fill the blank.
Rule 2. The word must make sense both to the sentence it is in and to the entire story.
Rule 3. The word you choose must be grammatically correct and spelled correctly.

Note: In the letter to the student, you read that you will need to think about what you are doing. Here is your opportunity to show what you already know about English.

AN UNDISCIPLINED SOLDIER

It was a very ___(1)___ day, and a soldier ___(2)___ in his tent was ___(3)___ tired and uncomfortable. The ___(4)___

had been at the _____ camp for a month, _____
(5)   (6)

nearly every day the _____ had to march, run, _____
(7)   (8)

climb. And now they _____ to go out into _____
(9)   (10)

desert to spend the _____ day in the hot _____
(11)   (12)

pretending to fight a _____ battle.
(13)

   One of the _____ was a lazy man _____
(14)   (15)

name was Robinson. He _____ got into trouble with _____
(16)   (17)

officer because he was _____ able to do anything _____
(18)   (19)

right way.

   On that _____ day, Robinson thought, "It's _____
(20)   (21)

very hot day today. _____ get very tired if _____
(22)   (23)

go out in the _____ with my unit to _____ to fight a battle.
(24)   (25)

_____ I don't think I'll _____."
(26)   (27)

   An hour later, when _____ soldiers passed a few _____
(28)   (29)

trees before they reached _____ desert, Robinson jumped behind
(30)

_____ of the trees and _____ until everyone passed by.
(31)   (32)

_____ he sat down in _____ shade and began to
(33)   (34)

_____ the book he had _____ with him.
(35)   (36)

   That evening, _____ the soldiers again passed _____
(37)   (38)

large trees, Robinson very _____ joined his unit again.
(39)

_____ had carefully put dust _____ his face and clothes
(40)   (41)

_____ that he would look _____ dirty as the others
(42)   (43)

_____ had spent the entire _____ crawling in the desert.
(44)   (45)

_____ the soldiers reached the _____,
(46)   (47)

the officer-in-charge _____ to tell each of _____
(48)   (49)

soldiers the mistakes they _____ made during the day.
(50)

" _____ we had fought a _____ enemy," he said, "nearly
(51)   (52)

_____ of you would be _____ now."
(53)   (54)

   The officer finally _____, "Robinson!"
(55)

Robinson was sure (56) _____ the officer realized that (57) _____ had been absent and (58) _____ he would be severely (59) _____. He stepped forward, trembling.

" (60) _____!" said the officer-in- (61) _____. "You were the only (62) _____ who I did not (63) _____ do anything wrong today."

Exercise 3.
EXAMINING THE FILLERS FOR THE CLOZE

Directions:

Look at the choices you have made for the blanks in your text as each person reads a sentence with the fillers he or she has chosen for the blanks. If your choice differs from the one you hear, and you are not sure if your answer is correct, ask your teacher to explain. Often there is more than one appropriate filler for the blank. Check to see whether you have spelled the word correctly and whether you have put the capital letters, periods, and other punctuation marks where they belong.

Exercise 4.
EXAMINATION OF PREDICTIONS

Directions:

As you and your class go over each prediction that you made earlier, you are going to decide whether the statement is *implicit, explicit,* or *unknown,* based on the story you have just read. Be sure to ask your teacher if these words are not clear to you. As you read each prediction, think about what you have read in the story and then decide. It will often be necessary to go back to the text and find justification for your answer.

Exercise 5.
READER RESPONSE SHEET

Directions:

Please answer the following questions in complete sentences.

Example:

1. How did the soldier feel on that hot day?
   The soldier felt tired and uncomfortable on that hot day.

2. How did the soldiers spend their days? Why?

_____

_____

_____

_____

_____

3. Why didn't the soldier want to participate in the battle drills?

_____

_____

_____

4. What do you think of the soldier's plan to avoid the drills?

_____

_____

5. What are some questions that you have about the story?

Example:

Where did the soldier find a book in the desert?

_____

_____

_____

_____

_____

_____

_____

6. What are some words or expressions that are not clear to you?

_____   _____   _____

_____   _____   _____

7. What two things did you find out from doing the cloze, and how are you going to practice them? Please be specific.

_____

_____

_____

_____

_____

_____

_____

Exercise 6.
COMPREHENSION/DISCUSSION QUESTIONS

Directions:

Please read the following questions. Discuss them with your peers, and then write the answers in complete sentences.

Example:

1. What kind of person is the soldier?
   The soldier is a lazy person.

2. What do you think of the place where the soldiers did their drills? Why is it necessary to hold battle drills in isolated areas?

_____

_____

_____

_____

3. Would you like to spend your time doing such exercises? Why? Why not?

_____

_____

_____

_____

_____

4. If you were the soldier, what kind of plan would you formulate?

_____

_____

_____

_____

_____

5. Why is it necessary for the army to maintain discipline?

_____

_____

_____

_____

6. Is discipline necessary in other areas of life? Why? Why not?

_____

_____

_____

_____

7. Why was it particularly difficult to maintain discipline in the desert?

_____

_____

_____

_____

_____

Exercise 7.
GRAMMAR POINT

Definite/Indefinite Article

The story of the soldier starts by talking about *a* soldier in the title and in the first sentence. The very next mention, however, is "The soldier." We're going to find out why we used *a* and *the* in these two cases.

A and *the* are articles. They are little words that are used before nouns in English, and each carries a particular meaning or message. *The* is a *definite article; a* is an *indefinite article.*

Form:

We use the indefinite article *a* before any singular noun that is not specific. For example, we can say:

> I need *a* chair. (any chair, the kind is not specified)
>
> We saw *a* movie. (the kind of movie is unknown, unspecified)

If we want to be specific and refer to something in particular, we need to use the definite article *the.* There are three main uses of the definite article:

1. The definite article *the* is used when we mean something specific that the listener or reader does not yet know about. This is called a *promissory use* of the definite article because we promise to give the audience more information.
For example:

> I need *the* chair.

I don't mean any chair but a particular one. I also need to convey more information so that the listener will know what I mean. Therefore, I say:

> I need *the* chair standing near the door.
>
> **Or:** I need *the* chair that is right behind you.

In the above examples, I have kept my promise to give the reader or listener more information about the specific chair I mean.

2. A second major use of the definite article *the* is to talk about something that we have already mentioned. We call this the *second mention* of the noun.

For example, the story started out talking about *a soldier.* The next time, the character in the story is referred to as *the* soldier. He had already been mentioned earlier in the story.

Similarly, when we speak to someone with whom we have gone to a movie, we say: How did you like *the* movie? The movie is now information that both the listener and the speaker share. Therefore, we use the definite article *the.*

3. The third important use of the definite article is as part of the name of countries beginning with the words *union* or *united*.

Examples:

    the Union of South Africa

    the United States

    the Union of Soviet Socialist Republics

Note: Although the *the* is part of the title, it is not capitalized.

We also use *the* before the names of certain places:

    the Holland Tunnel   *the* Museum of Natural History
    the Botanical Gardens   *the* United Nations

Again, the word *the* is not capitalized.

Directions:

Please read the following paragraph. Use the articles *a* or *the* in the appropriate places.

There are many rich people in _____ United States.

_____ rich person is one who lives in _____ big house, owns _____ beautiful, expensive car, and has _____ live-in maid.

_____ rich person who lives across _____ street from me is _____ kind person. Even though he is rich, he still drives _____ same car he drove two years ago, goes to _____ movies in our town, and shops in _____ local supermarket.

Now write your own paragraph using the definite and indefinite articles. Try to think about those times when you were not sure which to use and see whether you can become surer of your use of articles.

_____

_____

_____

_____

_____

_____

_____

Exercise 8.
WORD BUILDING

Count/Non-count Nouns

In English, we classify nouns in several different ways. There are count nouns and non-count nouns, or concrete and abstract nouns.

When we talk about count nouns, we mean those name words (nouns) that we can put a number in front of.

For example, we can say:

> one soldier, two soldiers
>
> one officer, three officers

Examples:

> The soldier had one gun.
>
> The soldier had two books.

We usually form the plural of count nouns by adding *s* to the end of the word.

unit → units	desert → deserts
day → days	battle → battles
plan → plans	

In words ending in *ch,* we add *es* to form the plural, as follows:

church → churches   inch → inches   branch → branches

Can you think of any additional examples that fit into this category?

_____   _____   _____

In words ending in *y*, we change the *y* to *i* and add *es*, as follows:

baby → babies   library → libraries

Now you think of some additional examples that belong here.

_____   _____   _____

Another rule for forming the plural is that we add *es* to singular nouns ending in *s, z, sh,* or *x.* Write some words that you can think of that fit this rule.

Example:
dish → dishes

_____   _____   _____

_____   _____   _____

In addition, you remember that in Unit 1, we talked about compound nouns like *haircut* and *barbershop.* We said then that these nouns form the plural as other count nouns in English do, namely: haircut*s*, barbershop*s*.

Finally, we sometimes refer to people who have special jobs or who are related to us by marriage in special ways. Their titles are editor-in-chief or officer-in-charge. Similarly, we refer to the family of our spouse as brother-in-law, sister-in-law, etc.

We form the plural of these words by adding *s* to the main noun.

editor*s*-in-chief   officer*s*-in-charge   son*s*-in-law

Now you think of some additional examples:

_____   _____   _____

All the variations we have spoken about for forming the plural of singular count nouns are regular. There are, however, some exceptions to the way we make some count nouns plural.

Examples:
man → men   woman → women

We should also note that in words ending in *man,* we form the plural by changing the *man* part: chairman → chairmen.

Here are some examples of irregular plurals of count nouns. These forms need to be memorized so that you can use them.

analysis	→ analyses	leaf	→ leaves	self	→ selves
child	→ children	loaf	→ loaves	shelf	→ shelves
foot	→ feet	man	→ men	tooth	→ teeth
half	→ halves	mouse	→ mice	wife	→ wives
knife	→ knives	potato	→ potatoes	woman	→ women

You probably know enough English by now to realize that the above is only a partial listing of the irregular plural forms in English. These are, however, some of the more commonly used plurals, and they indicate to you some of the patterns of these irregular forms.

Directions:

Write a paragraph in which you use as many singular and/or plural count noun forms as you can. Try to use some of the irregular forms as well. Your first sentence might look like this:

> **My friends and I formed a club. We meet on Saturday nights and Sunday afternoons.**

Or: **I have just joined a photography club at school. There are fourteen members in our group.**

_____

_____

_____

_____

_____

_____

_____

_____

Non-count nouns are those nouns that we do not put a number in front of. There are two kinds of non-count nouns:

1. mass nouns — Mass nouns are those nouns that refer to things like coffee, sugar, tea, hair, money.
2. abstract nouns — Abstract nouns are those nouns that refer to a quality, such as intelligence, patience, cruelty, beauty, laziness, happiness, kindness.

We do not put numbers in front of these nouns; therefore, in English, we don't say "*one* laziness or *one* patience"; neither do we usually use the word *the* in front of these nouns.

Example:

For the soldier, happiness meant avoiding army drills.

Directions:

We now have some guidelines for the use of count and non-count nouns. Let's see how we can apply the information to our writing. Write a paragraph in which you use both count and non-count nouns to describe your interest in something special. Your first sentences might look like this:

Health, happiness and safety are major concerns of government leaders and scientists all over the world. Both scientists and government leaders realize that millions of dollars are needed to clean up the pollution in the air.

_____

_____

_____

_____

_____

_____

Exercise 9.
WRITING ACTIVITIES

Directions:

Please read the following suggested topics. Then choose one topic and write about it.

1. Rewrite the story in your own words. See whether you can write it from the officer's point of view. You might start like this:

Last year I was in charge of a unit in the desert. It was very hot, and it was often difficult for the soldiers to do the required drills.

2. Choose a partner and together write a dialogue describing the soldier's report of how he managed to take a day off from drilling. **Or:** Write a dialogue describing the officer talking to his colleague explaining the difficulty of maintaining discipline among the soldiers under his command in the desert.

3. What kind of person was the officer-in-charge? What was the chief difference between the officer and Robinson? Were you ever in a situation where you had to discipline yourself to do something you really didn't want to do? How did you handle it? Write about it. Of course, you realize that you are free to make up your own story, so be creative.

4. Army officers need to maintain discipline among the soldiers under their command. Not only is discipline necessary in the army, but it is also needed by students, teachers, parents, and workers.

Do you agree or disagree?

Write an essay the very best way you can. Use your knowledge of the world, what you have read, and/or what you have studied to support your point of view.

5. Please choose your own topic and write about it.

Exercise 10.
DICTATION

Directions:

Your teacher will dictate the following sentences to you. Your job is to write them as accurately as you can. As you write your sentences, remember to use correct spelling and punctuation. Finally, even if you don't hear every word clearly, try to use all the clues in the sentence to help you figure out the difficult word. Do what you have practiced in the doing of the cloze.

1. A soldier was tired and uncomfortable in the desert.
2. He and his unit drilled in the desert nearly every day.
3. The unit marched, ran, and climbed in the heat.
4. Robinson wanted to avoid the daily drill.
5. Robinson hid behind one of the tall trees.
6. The soldier read his book while his unit drilled.
7. In the evening Robinson put dust on his face and clothes.
8. Then he joined the soldiers in his unit.
9. The officer-in-charge criticized all the soldiers.
10. Robinson was the only soldier who had done nothing wrong.

Unit 5
THE APPROPRIATENESS OF KNOWLEDGE

Exercise 1.
MAKING PREDICTIONS (DRTA)

Directions:

Read the title of the cloze that your teacher has written on the board. Based on the information that you see on the board, see how many predictions you can make about the story that you are about to read.

We are going to complete this sentence:

We're going to find out . . .

Example:

1. We're going to find out what appropriate knowledge means.

Now you and your peers will think of additional predictions as one of your classmates writes them on the board.

_____

_____

_____

_____

_____

_____

_____

_____

_____

_____

_____

_____

_____

_____

_____

_____

Exercise 2.
DOING THE CLOZE

Directions:

Read the entire passage to yourself first. Do not try to fill the blanks before you have completed reading the story. When you have finished reading, you are ready to start working with the other members of your group to fill the blanks. Together, you are going to decide on appropriate fillers for each of the blanks.

There are three rules that you need to remember:

Rule 1. You can use only *one* word to fill the blank.
Rule 2. The word must make sense both to the sentence it is in and to the entire story.
Rule 3. The word you choose must be grammatically correct and spelled correctly.

Note: In the letter to the student, you read that you will need to think about what you are doing. Here is your opportunity to show what you already know about English.

THE APPROPRIATENESS OF KNOWLEDGE

Mr. Smith was a _____ at a university. He _____
(1)   (2)
a lot of foreign _____ and lectured about them _____
(3)   (4)
his students. He was _____ very proud man and _____
(5)   (6)
that people who did _____ know a lot of _____
(7)   (8)
were stupid and useless. _____ was never tired of _____
(9)   (10)
this to anybody whom _____ met.
(11)

One day during _____ summer holidays, Mr. Smith
(12)
_____ traveling in a foreign _____ and studying
(13)   (14)
the languages _____ were spoken there. He _____
(15)   (16)
much wanted to visit _____ fishing village where an _____
(17)   (18)
language was spoken, but _____ was on an island _____
(19)   (20)
the middle of a _____ lake, so he had _____ find a boat to
(21)   (22)
_____ him across.
(23)

It was _____ easy, but at last _____
(24)   (25)
found a fisherman with _____ very small, very narrow
(26)
_____ who was ready to _____ him across the lake
(27)   (28)
_____ the island.
(29)

While the _____ was rowing the boat _____,
(30)   (31)
Mr. Smith said to _____, "How many languages do _____
(32)   (33)
know?"

"How many languages?" _____ poor fisherman answered. "I
(34)
_____ only one. I don't _____ to know more. I'm
(35)   (36)
_____ a poor fisherman."
(37)

"If _____ know only one language," _____
(38)   (39)
Mr. Smith, "half your _____ is worth nothing."
(40)

The _____ said nothing.
(41)

When the _____ was about a mile _____ the shore of the
(42)   (43)

_____ (44), a strong wind suddenly _____ (45) to blow. The small

_____ (46) began to roll, and _____ (47) began to come in

_____ (48) the sides.

"Sir," said _____ (49) fisherman, "do you know _____ (50) to swim?"

"No, I _____ (51) not," answered Mr. Smith.

" _____ (52) you do not know _____ (53) to swim," said the

_____ (54), "not only half your _____ (55) but your whole life

_____ (56) worth nothing because we're _____ (57) to sink very soon."

Exercise 3.
EXAMINING THE FILLERS FOR THE CLOZE

Directions:

Look at the choices you have made for the blanks in your text as each person reads a sentence with the fillers he or she has chosen for the blanks. If your choice differs from the one you hear, and you are not sure if your answer is correct, ask your teacher to explain. Often there is more than one appropriate filler for the blank. Check to see whether you have spelled the word correctly and whether you have put the capital letters, periods, and other punctuation marks where they belong.

Exercise 4.
EXAMINATION OF PREDICTIONS

Directions:

As you and your class go over each prediction that you made earlier, you are going to decide whether the statement is *implicit, explicit,* or *unknown,* based on the story you have just read. Be sure to ask your teacher if these words are not clear to you. As you read each prediction, think about what you have read in the story and then decide. It will often be necessary to go back to the text and find justification for your answer.

Exercise 5.
READER RESPONSE SHEET

Directions:

Please answer the following questions in complete sentences.

Example:

1. Why did the author write the story?
   The author wrote the story to tell us about the foolishness of a person.

2. What did Mr. Smith do for a living?

   _____

   _____

3. Why was it difficult for him to do his research?

   _____

   _____

   _____

   _____

4. How did he manage to overcome that difficulty?

   _____

   _____

   _____

   _____

   _____

5. What happened as they were rowing across the lake?

   _____

   _____

   _____

   _____

   _____

6. What questions do you have about the story?

Example:

Why did Mr. Smith think the fisherman was stupid?

_____

_____

_____

_____

_____

_____

_____

7. What words and/or expressions are not clear to you?

_____   _____   _____

_____   _____   _____

8. What two things did you learn from doing this cloze, and how are you
   going to practice them? Please be specific.

_____

_____

_____

_____

_____

Exercise 6.
COMPREHENSION/DISCUSSION QUESTIONS

Directions:

Please read the following questions. Discuss them with your peers, and
then write the answers in complete sentences.

Example:

1. What kind of person is Mr. Smith?
   Mr. Smith is an arrogant person.

2. How do you know?

_____

_____

3. Why was Mr. Smith interested in going to that particular island?

_____

_____

4. What was Mr. Smith's attitude toward the fisherman? How do you know?

_____

_____

_____

5. Why do you think it is important to do research on languages?

_____

_____

_____

_____

6. Are you interested in doing that kind of research? Why? Why not?

_____

_____

_____

_____

_____

7. What do you think of people who can speak more than one language?

_____

_____

_____

_____

8. What do people in the United States and in your country think about studying foreign languages?

Exercise 7.
GRAMMAR POINT

True Conditional

When we want to talk about something that is true if another thing is true, we call that a *true conditional*. That is, one situation or occurrence is dependent on or hinges on another. The end result, however, is a true statement.

Here are a few examples:

If the weather is warm, we go swimming.

(We need warm weather in order to go swimming. If it isn't warm, we can't go swimming.)

If the fisherman catches fish, he is happy.

(The fisherman sells his fish, gets money, and then he is happy.)

If he can't swim, the lecturer's life isn't worth anything.

(The boat is full of water. The lecturer can't swim. He'll drown.)

Conditional sentences can be written in two ways.

1. If he can't find a boat, he can't do his research.
2. He can't do his research if he can't find a boat.

Did you find the difference between sentences 1 and 2?
Yes, you're right. Sentence 1 has a comma, while sentence 2 does not.

The reason that there is no comma in sentence 2 is that there is no interruption in the word order.

He can't do his research.
S   V   O

There is no *if* that comes in front of the subject.

We can also describe the true conditional in the following way: We can see that one part of the sentence is the cause (the *if* part), and the other part is what happens as a result of that cause. Often the effect will occur in the future as a result of some other event, and, therefore, we use the simple present for the cause part (the *if* part) and the future for the effect (the result part).

Examples:

> If he can't swim, the lecturer will drown.
>
> (The cause, the *if* part, is that the lecturer can't swim. The *effect* is that he will drown.)
>
> The fisherman will be happy if he catches fish.
>
> (Here, again, we use the future to indicate that as a result of catching fish, the fisherman will be happy.)

Now let's think of some additional examples:

> If we study English, we learn.
>
> We can continue our college studies if we know English.

Directions:

People often use the word *if* when they talk or write about events in their lives. See how many situations you can think of. If you feel you can write a paragraph, please do so. Otherwise write ten sentences. You might start with the following:

> **If I know English, I'll be able to take regular courses.**

1. _____

2. _____

_____

3. _____

_____

4. _____

_____

5. _____

_____

6. _____

_____

7. _____

_____

8. _____

_____

9. _____

_____

10. _____

_____

Perhaps you could write a paragraph that would begin like this:

If I know English, I can do many things. I can get a job in an office instead of in a factory if I know English.

_____

_____

_____

_____

Exercise 8.
WORD BUILDING

Quantifiers

There are times when we don't want to indicate the exact amount of whatever it is we're talking about. For example, we might say, "I need some time." In this case, we do not specify the exact amount of time required. Or we might ask, "Do you have some money?" Here again, we are requesting an unspecified amount of money.

The following words are called *quantifiers*. They are used to indicate non-specific amounts.

a few/few	some/several	a great deal of/a lot of
a little/little	much/many	

We have already learned about count and non-count nouns. The use of the above words depends on whether they are followed by singular or plural count nouns or by non-count nouns.

Example:
We can say,

> Mr. Smith knew a lot of languages.
>
> (We don't know exactly how many.)

Or: Mr. Smith asked several fishermen to take him across the lake.

(The exact number of fishermen is unknown.)

Here are some rules and examples to help you in your use of these words:

Rule 1. *Few/a few* are used with *count* nouns. *A few* has a *positive* meaning → several. *Few* has a *negative* meaning → almost no one.

Example:

Although there were *a few* fishermen in the fishing village, Mr. Smith had *few* offers to take him across the lake.

Now write your own examples using *few/a few.*

_____

_____

_____

_____

_____

_____

Rule 2.   *Much/many* are used to indicate more than two or three of something, a lot. *Much* is used with *non-count* nouns. *Many* is used with *count* nouns.

Examples:

Doing research requires *much* work. It also requires *much* effort.

Speakers of *many* languages have access to a variety of people and cultures.

Mr. Smith had to work *many* hours to get his data.

Now write your own examples using *much/many.*

_____

_____

_____

_____

_____

Rule 3.   *A great deal of/a lot of* are similar in meaning. They are *not* similar in use. *A great deal of* is used with *non-count* nouns. *A lot of* is used with both *count* and *non-count* nouns.

Examples:

a. Doing research takes *a great deal of* time. It also often takes *a great deal of* money. (What kinds of nouns are these?)

Or:

> b. Doing research takes *a lot of* time and money. (You notice we used both *a great deal of* and *a lot of* with these non-count nouns.)

In addition, *a lot of* can also be used with count nouns.

Example:
> Research often takes the effort of *a lot of* investigators.

Note: We cannot say: Research often takes the effort of *a great deal of* investigators.

Now write your own examples using *a great deal of* and *a lot of.*

_____

_____

_____

_____

_____

_____

Directions:

Look at the examples you have written above. Choose some of these sentences and combine them in a paragraph using these quantifiers correctly. You might start with the following sentence:

Many students of English as a second language spend a lot of time on their studies.

_____

_____

_____

_____

_____

_____

_____

_____

_____

_____

_____

Exercise 9.
WRITING ACTIVITIES

Directions:

Please read the following suggested topics. Then choose one topic and write about it.

1. Rewrite the story in your own words. You may wish to write it from the fisherman's point of view.

   Your story might start like this:

   Some time ago, a university professor came to my village.

2. Choose a partner. Write a dialogue in which you describe to your friend the experience you, the fisherman, had with the university professor. Or you might write a dialogue in which you describe the experience that you, the professor, had with the fisherman.

3. How do you feel about the way the professor treated the fisherman? Did you ever have that kind of experience? How did you feel then? How do you feel about it now?

   Write about your experience. Describe the complete situation telling the reader what happened, when it happened, where it happened, how it happened, and, if you know the reason, why it happened. If you are fortunate enough never to have had that kind of experience, please make one up.

4. Whatever we, as human beings, know is important information, and we never know when we can make use of that information. There is no reason to think that one kind of knowledge or skill is better than another. Every kind of knowledge is important. There is no such thing as better or worse knowledge.

Do you agree or disagree?

Write an essay the very best way you can. Use your knowledge of the world, what you have read, and/or what you have studied to support your point of view.

5. Please choose your own topic and write about it.

Exercise 10.
DICTATION

Directions:

Your teacher will dictate the following sentences to you. Your job is to write them as accurately as you can. As you write your sentences, remember to use correct spelling and punctuation. Finally, even if you don't hear every word clearly, try to use all the clues in the sentence to help you figure out the difficult word. Do what you have practiced in the doing of the cloze.

1. Mr. Smith is a university professor of languages.
2. He knows many languages and lectures about them.
3. He sets out to do research on an unusual language one day.
4. Those language speakers live on an island across the lake.
5. If he wants to cross the lake, he needs a fisherman and a boat.
6. A fisherman finally agrees to take him where he wants to go.
7. A storm begins on their way across the lake.
8. Mr. Smith thinks it's important to know many languages.
9. The fisherman thinks it's important to know how to swim.
10. If Mr. Smith can't swim, he will certainly drown.

Unit 6
AN HONEST ACTOR

Exercise 1.
MAKING PREDICTIONS (DRTA)

Directions:

Read the title of the cloze that your teacher has written on the board. Based on the information that you see on the board, see how many predictions you can make about the story that you are about to read.

We are going to complete this sentence:

We're going to find out . . .

Example:

1. We're going to find out whether the actor was male or female.

Now you and your peers will think of additional predictions as one of your classmates writes them on the board.

_____

_____

_____

_____

_____

_____

_____

_____

_____

_____

_____

_____

_____

_____

_____

_____

Exercise 2.
DOING THE CLOZE

Directions:

Read the entire passage to yourself first. Do not try to fill the blanks before you have completed reading the story. When you have finished reading, you are ready to start working with the other members of your group to fill the blanks. Together, you are going to decide on appropriate fillers for each of the blanks.

There are three rules that you need to remember:

Rule 1.   You can use only *one* word to fill the blank.
Rule 2.   The word must make sense both to the sentence it is in and to the entire story.
Rule 3.   The word you choose must be grammatically correct and spelled correctly.

Note: In the letter to the student, you read that you will need to think about what you are doing. Here is your opportunity to show what you already know about English.

AN HONEST ACTOR

Jack was an actor _____ (1) a small seaside town. _____ (2)
lived in a small _____ (3) in a house that _____ (4)
owned by an old _____ (5) whose name was Ms. _____ (6).
He never had much _____ (7), so he always found _____ (8)
difficult to pay Ms. _____ (9) the rent for his _____ (10).
    Then one week, the _____ (11) in which he worked _____ (12),
and he was not _____ (13) to find another job, _____ (14)
he had no money _____ (15) the rent at all. _____ (16)
decided to go to _____ (17) town to try to _____ (18)
another job, but he _____ (19) that if he tried _____ (20)
leave the house with _____ (21) luggage before he paid _____ (22)
rent, Ms. Jenkins would _____ (23) the police, so he _____ (24)
one of his friends _____ (25) help him to escape _____ (26)
her house.
    Jack put _____ (27) his bathing trunks, packed _____ (28)
the rest of his _____ (29) except a towel in _____ (30)
suitcase and dropped the _____ (31) out of a window. _____ (32)
friend, who was waiting _____ (33), took the suitcase down
_____ (34) the beach, while Jack _____ (35) past Ms. Jenkins and
_____ (36) of the house in _____ (37) bathing trunks with his
_____ (38) over his shoulder. Of _____ (39), she thought that he
_____ (40) going for a swim. _____ (41) went down to the
_____ (42), opened the suitcase that _____ (43) friend had brought,
changed _____ (44) his clothes, and left.
    _____ (45) soon found a job _____ (46) his new home, and
_____ (47) three years he was _____ (48) and successful, so he
_____ (49) to go back and _____ (50) Ms. Jenkins the money
_____ (51) he owed her.

At (52) _____ Ms. Jenkins did not (53) _____ him in his beautiful, (54) _____ suit. When at last (55) _____ realized that it was (56) _____, she was very surprised.

"(57) _____ God!" she cried. "I (58) _____ that you had drowned."

Exercise 3.
EXAMINING THE FILLERS FOR THE CLOZE

Directions:

Look at the choices you have made for the blanks in your text as each person reads a sentence with the fillers he or she has chosen for the blanks. If your choice differs from the one you hear, and you are not sure if your answer is correct, ask your teacher to explain. Often there is more than one appropriate filler for the blank. Check to see whether you have spelled the word correctly and whether you have put the capital letters, periods, and other punctuation marks where they belong.

Exercise 4.
EXAMINATION OF PREDICTIONS

Directions:

As you and your class go over each prediction that you made earlier, you are going to decide whether the statement is *implicit, explicit,* or *unknown,* based on the story you have just read. Be sure to ask your teacher if these words are not clear to you. As you read each prediction, think about what you have read in the story and then decide. It will often be necessary to go back to the text and find justification for your answer.

Exercise 5.
READER RESPONSE SHEET

Directions:

Please answer the following questions in complete sentences.

Example:

1. Do you think Jack did the right thing by leaving Ms. Jenkins's house as he did and when he did?
   Yes. I think Jack did the right thing.

2. Why didn't Ms. Jenkins pay any attention to Jack as he walked past her?

_____

_____

_____

3. Was Jack able to escape on his own or did he need help?

_____

_____

4. How did he escape from the house?

_____

_____

_____

_____

_____

5. What happened to him after he left that house?

_____

_____

_____

_____

6. What are some questions that you have about the story?

_____

_____

_____

_____

_____

7. What new words have you learned?

_____   _____   _____

_____   _____   _____

8. What words and/or expressions are still not clear to you?

_____   _____   _____

_____   _____   _____

9. What two things have you learned from doing this cloze, and how are you going to practice them? Please be specific.

_____

_____

_____

_____

_____

_____

_____

_____

Exercise 6.
COMPREHENSION/DISCUSSION QUESTIONS

Directions:

Please read the following questions. Discuss them with your peers, and then write the answers in complete sentences.

Example:

1. Why do actors often have little money?
   Actors often have little money because they don't work regularly.

2. How do many actors prepare for the time when they are unemployed?

_____

_____

_____

_____

3. How do you think Jack felt about not being able to pay the rent? How do you know?

_____

_____

_____

_____

_____

4. How would you have felt if you hadn't been able to pay the rent?

_____

_____

_____

_____

5. What kind of plan did Jack invent for leaving the house?

_____

_____

_____

_____

6. Using all the information in the story, describe Jack. Is he the kind of person you might like to meet? Why? Why not?

_____

_____

_____

_____

_____

7. What do you think of Jack's plan? Do you think you would have done what Jack did? Why? Why not?

_____

_____

_____

_____

_____

_____

_____

_____

Exercise 7.
GRAMMAR POINT

Untrue Conditional or Contrary-to-Fact

We often want to express the idea that if we knew something or did something or had something, something else would happen. The truth is, however, that we don't know or have something, and so the result is not going to happen.

Example:

> If we knew English well, we would not be in this class. The truth is that we don't know English well, and therefore we are in this class to learn.

That's what we mean by *contrary-to-fact*. The fact is that we don't know English well, and, because of that, we are in this class.

Form:

The form of the untrue conditional or contrary-to-fact is as follows:

If + subject + verb (past) + complement, + subject + would + base form of verb
If + Jack + had + money, + he + would + pay + the rent

Therefore, even though we are not talking about the past, we use the past tense of the verb in writing about the *untrue conditional,* or *contrary-to-fact.*

Now let's think of some additional examples to fit our formula or pattern for the *untrue conditional,* or *contrary-to-fact.*

> If I knew English well, I would not need this class.
>   wouldn't

If he went to the party, he would meet some nice people.
he'd

Are you paying attention to the fact that we have shortened the *would not* to *wouldn't* and the *he would* to *he'd*? How do you think we're going to shorten *I would, you would,* and *they would*? You're right. We use the same form for each of them, and we get the following:

I'd/we'd

you'd (singular)/you'd (plural)

he'd, she'd/they'd

We don't usually say *it'd*. If you try to pronounce it, you'll realize how awkward that pronunciation is. So we say the full two words: *it would*.

In addition, we need to note the forms of the verb *to be*, which, as we already know, behave differently from other verbs.

1. If Jack *were* rich, he wouldn't need to work.
2. If we *were* from South America, we'd probably speak Spanish.
3. If they *were* in San Francisco, they'd know about earthquakes.

Sentences 1, 2, and 3 can also be written as follows:

1. Jack wouldn't need to work if he *were* rich.
2. We'd probably speak Spanish if we *were* from South America.
3. They'd know about earthquakes if they *were* in San Francisco.

Can you tell the difference between the two groups of sentences? Right. The first group of sentences has a comma after the *if part,* as we have already learned. When we turn the sentence around and use the *if part* at the end, there is no need for a comma. However, we need to remember *to change the tense of the verb* in the *if part* of the sentence and to use the word *would* in the other part. Thus, the *if,* the *change in tense,* and the *would* are our clues to the *untrue conditional,* or *contrary-to-fact,* in the present.

Directions:

Now write your own contrary-to-fact paragraph telling about something that is not true but that you would surely like to be true.

You might start in the following way:

> **If my dream came true, I would be . . .**
>
> Or: **If I had all the time I want/need, I would . . .**

_____

_____

_____

_____

_____

_____

_____

_____

Exercise 8.
WORD BUILDING

Word Endings for Occupations

In this exercise, we are going to work on words like *actor, singer, painter*. Since you know the meanings of these words, can you guess what the ending of each word signifies?

Yes, you're right. The ending *er* or *or* means *one who*. A singer is one who sings. A painter is one who paints. And an actor is _____

_____ _____.

Here are some other words that follow the same pattern:

adviser	beginner	builder
contractor	dancer	driver
editor	negotiator	prompter
publisher	teacher	

There are other words in English that follow another pattern, and they are similar to the *er/or* pattern in that these endings also denote someone who does some particular job.

Here are some examples:

cellist	dentist	harpist
machinist	philanthropist	pianist
psychiatrist	psychologist	sociologist
taxidermist		

It is interesting to note the categories or groups that these words fall into. Can you figure out what those categories are? _____ and _____.

Can you think of any other words that relate to what a person does to earn his or her living?

Please choose some of the words from this exercise and write your own passage or story about people in different jobs or professions. You might start your passage in the following way:

There are many different colleges in the United States. Some colleges specialize in training people to work in the social sciences. They educate people to become sociologists, psychologists, etc.

Now finish it.

_____

_____

_____

_____

_____

_____

Exercise 9.
WRITING ACTIVITIES

Directions:

Please read the following suggested topics. Then choose one topic and write about it.

1. Rewrite the story in your own words. This time, however, you might want to tell it from Ms. Jenkins's point of view. You might start like this:

A funny thing happened in my rooming house a few days ago. An old tenant of mine came back to pay the rent he owed me.

2. Write about an experience you had in which you devised a plan for dealing with a difficult situation in your life. Tell about the situation and the strategies you used to solve the difficulty.

3. There are many professions that demand a lot of sacrifice and hard work on the part of those who wish to enter them and be successful in those particular fields. Choose two professions with which you are familiar; perhaps you are even interested in entering one of them. Write about the difficulties involved in entering those fields. For example, you might write about becoming a news reporter or an accountant.

4. The lives of actors are very tough. They are often unemployed for long periods of time. They may feel personally rejected because of the keen competition, which keeps many people unemployed. On the other hand, those who succeed often do become rich and famous.

I believe that the fame and fortune that may come with acting are not worth all the problems that actors face. I prefer a normal life, a steady job and income, and a 9 to 5 existence.

Do you agree or disagree?

Write an essay the very best way you can. Use your knowledge of the world, what you have read, and/or what you have studied to support your point of view.

5. Please choose your own topic and write about it.

Exercise 10.
DICTATION

Directions:

Your teacher will dictate the following sentences to you. Your job is to write them as accurately as you can. As you write your sentences, remember to use correct spelling and punctuation. Finally, even if you don't hear every word clearly, try to use all the clues in the sentence to help you figure out the difficult word. Do what you have practiced in the doing of the cloze.

1. Jack was an actor in a small town.
2. Jack was a roomer in Ms. Jenkins's house.

3. If he had money, he would pay the rent.
4. One day Jack's theater closed, and Jack had no money for rent.
5. He decided to leave the small town.
6. If he left without paying, Ms. Jenkins would call the police.
7. He packed his suitcase and threw it out the window.
8. He pretended he was going for a swim.
9. Instead he went to another town and became a builder.
10. Three years later he returned to pay Ms. Jenkins the rent.

Unit 7
A CURIOUS BORDER GUARD

Exercise 1.
MAKING PREDICTIONS (DRTA)

Directions:

Read the title of the cloze that your teacher has written on the board. Based on the information that you see on the board, see how many predictions you can make about the story that you are about to read.

We are going to complete this sentence:

We're going to find out . . .

Example:

1. We're going to find out where the guard worked.

Now you and your peers will think of additional predictions as one of your classmates writes them on the board.

_____

_____

_____

_____

_____

_____

_____

_____

_____

_____

_____

_____

_____

_____

_____

_____

_____

Exercise 2.
DOING THE CLOZE

Directions:

Read the entire passage to yourself first. Do not try to fill the blanks before you have completed reading the story. When you have finished reading, you are ready to start working with the other members of your group to fill the blanks. Together, you are going to decide on appropriate fillers for each of the blanks.

There are three rules that you need to remember:

Rule 1. You can use only *one* word to fill the blank.
Rule 2. The word must make sense both to the sentence it is in and to the entire story.
Rule 3. The word you choose must be grammatically correct and spelled correctly.

Note: In the letter to the student, you read that you will need to think about what you are doing. Here is your opportunity to show what you already know about English.

A CURIOUS BORDER GUARD

Henry's job was to ___(1)___ cars that crossed the ___(2)___ to make sure that ___(3)___ were not smuggling anything ___(4)___ the country without paying.

___(5)___ evening except on weekends, ___(6)___ used to see a ___(7)___ worker coming up the ___(8)___ toward the frontier, pushing ___(9)___ bicycle with a big ___(10)___ of old straw on ___(11)___. When the bicycle reached ___(12)___ frontier, Henry used to ___(13)___ the man and make ___(14)___ take the straw off ___(15)___ untie it. Then he ___(16)___ to examine the straw ___(17)___ carefully to see whether ___(18)___ could find anything. After ___(19)___ he used to look ___(20)___ all the man's pockets. ___(21)___ he let him tie ___(22)___ straw up again, put ___(23)___ on his bicycle, and ___(24)___ off down the hill ___(25)___ it. Although Henry was ___(26)___ expecting to find gold, ___(27)___ jewelry, or other valuable ___(28)___ hidden in the straw, ___(29)___ never found anything, even ___(30)___ he examined it very ___(31)___. He was sure that ___(32)___ man was smuggling something, ___(33)___ he was not able ___(34)___ imagine what it could ___(35)___.

Then one evening, after ___(36)___ had looked through the ___(37)___ and emptied the factory ___(38)___ pockets as carefully as ___(39)___ always did, he said ___(40)___ him, "Listen, I know ___(41)___ you're smuggling things across ___(42)___ frontier. Won't you tell ___(43)___ what it is that ___(44)___ bringing into the country ___(45)___ successfully? I'm an old ___(46)___, and today's my last ___(47)___ in this job. Tomorrow ___(48)___ going to retire. I ___(49)___

that I shall not _____ anyone else if you _____
(50)   (51)
what you've been smuggling."

_____ factory worker did not _____
(52)   (53)
anything for some time. _____ he smiled, turned slowly
(54)
_____ Henry, and said quietly, " _____."
(55)   (56)

Exercise 3.
EXAMINING THE FILLERS FOR THE CLOZE

Directions:

Look at the choices you have made for the blanks in your text as each person reads a sentence with the fillers he or she has chosen for the blanks. If your choice differs from the one you hear, and you are not sure if your answer is correct, ask your teacher to explain. Often there is more than one appropriate filler for the blank. Check to see whether you have spelled the word correctly and whether you have put the capital letters, periods, and other punctuation marks where they belong.

Exercise 4.
EXAMINATION OF PREDICTIONS

Directions:

As you and your class go over each prediction that you made earlier, you are going to decide whether the statement is *implicit, explicit,* or *unknown,* based on the story you have just read. Be sure to ask your teacher if these words are not clear to you. As you read each prediction, think about what you have read in the story and then decide. It will often be necessary to go back to the text and find justification for your answer.

Exercise 5.
READER RESPONSE SHEET

Directions:

Please answer the following questions in complete sentences.

Example:

1. Were you surprised by the ending of the story?
    Yes, I was very surprised by the ending of the story.

2. Would you have told the border guard your secret? Why? Why not?

_____

_____

_____

3. Do you think Henry was a good border guard? Why? Why not?

_____

_____

_____

4. What are some questions that you have about the story?

Example:

Why was the border guard so suspicious?

_____

_____

_____

_____

_____

_____

_____

5. Which words and/or expressions are still not clear to you even though you have examined the context carefully?

_____   _____   _____

_____   _____   _____

6. What two things did you learn from doing this cloze, and how are you going to practice them? Please be specific.

_____

_____

_____

_____

_____

_____

_____

_____

Exercise 6.
COMPREHENSION/DISCUSSION QUESTIONS

Directions:

Please read the following questions. Discuss them with your peers, and then write the answers in complete sentences.

Example:

1. Why is it necessary for a country to have border guards?
    It is necessary to have border guards to check everybody who crosses the border.

2. Do you think the new Soviet approach to *glasnost* has changed the need for border guards? Why? Why not?

    _____

    _____

    _____

3. What kind of men were Henry and the factory worker? Please describe them as fully as you can.

    _____

    _____

    _____

    _____

4. Do you think Henry was a good border guard? Do you think the factory worker would have been a good border guard? Why? Why not?

    _____

    _____

_____

_____

5. If you were the factory worker, would you have revealed your secret to Henry? Why? Why not?

_____

_____

_____

_____

6. If you were the president of the world, would you have guards on the borders of different countries? Why? Why not?

_____

_____

_____

_____

7. Why was the factory worker able to steal the bicycles without getting caught?

_____

_____

_____

_____

_____

Exercise 7.
GRAMMAR POINT

Used To

Used to is a structure that refers to an activity that was true in the past and that often happened regularly in the past but is no longer true. We often use *any more* with *used to*.

Examples:

> Henry *used to* examine those who crossed the border every day. Now that he is retired, he doesn't do it *any more*.

> Jack *used to* have trouble paying the rent to Ms. Jenkins. Now that he is rich, he doesn't have that problem *any more*.

Directions:

Think about where you used to live or what you used to do before you came to the United States. Write a few paragraphs describing life in your country. (If you wish, you may write on any other topic.) You might start your paragraph like this:

In my country, I used to live in a small house. I used to shop in the store at the corner. Although it was a small store, they used to sell most of the items I needed.

Once a week I used to go downtown. I used to shop in a department store. I used to ride in a trolley car. On my way there and back home, I used to pass beautiful apartment houses.

I don't do these things any more. Now I shop in a large supermarket, and I live in an ugly apartment house.

_____

_____

_____

_____

_____

_____

_____

_____

_____

_____

Form:

In addition, in Unit 3 we learned about the structure *used to* meaning to be accustomed to something. For example, when I first came to the United States, I was not *used to seeing* such tall buildings. I was not *used to* the transportation system, and I often got lost. Nowadays, everything is fine. I am *used to living* in this country.

Rule 1. *Used to* + base form of verb + *ing* is the formula we need for this additional meaning of *used to*.

Examples:

I was not used to seeing such tall buildings.

I was not used to riding in crowded trains.

Rule 2. *Used to* + noun is the formula we need to indicate being accustomed to something or someone.

Examples:

I am now used to public transportation.

I am used to my new school.

Directions:

Think about some of the things that you had to get used to when you first came to the United States. Then write a paragraph about your experiences. You might like to combine both meanings of this structure in your paragraph.

You might start with a sentence like this:

Before I came to this country, I used to live in a small town. It was hard to get used to a large apartment house.

_____

_____

_____

_____

_____

_____

_____

_____

Exercise 8.
WORD BUILDING

Nouns as Adjectives

In Unit 1, we learned several ways to make new words in English. We learned that we can combine two nouns to form one word — *notebook*. We can also combine a noun and a verb to form a new word — *haircut*. An additional way of building new words is to combine a preposition and a noun — *outlaw*. We can also combine a preposition and a verb to form a noun — *bypass*.

Yet another way to create new words is to combine two nouns and use the first one as an adjective.

For example, if we take the two nouns *vegetable* and *store*, we can use them to indicate the particular store in which vegetables are sold. In this case, the word *vegetable* is used as an adjective to show the special kind of store we mean. From this pattern of noun functioning as adjective + noun, we get new nouns like *apartment house, department store, factory worker,* and *communist meetings*.

In our example, *vegetable store*, we made a new term that we can add to our vocabulary by combining the noun with the noun. Similarly, we can make other noun + noun combinations into new words. For example, from *scholarship + fund*, we get a particular kind of fund, a *scholarship fund*, or from *desk + drawer*, we get *desk drawer*, a drawer that belongs to a desk.

To form the plural of these noun + noun combinations, we add *s* to the second noun only. A *scholarship fund* becomes *scholarship funds*; a *desk drawer* becomes *desk drawers*.

When you write, be sure to check yourself to see that you have observed the plural rule correctly.

The following is a list of some nouns. See how creative you can be by combining two nouns to form new words. Draw a line from the word in column A that goes with the word in column B.

A	B
picture	chair
nail	course
desk	cleaner
science	furniture
language	book
living-room	speaker
window	polish

Directions:

Now use your new words to write a paragraph about something that is interesting to you and that you'd like to share with others.

Your paragraph might start like this:

I had studied about the Swiss Alps in my science course. When I went to Canada last year, I . . .

Exercise 9.
WRITING ACTIVITIES

Directions:

Please read the following suggested topics. Then choose one topic and write about it.

1. Rewrite the story in your own words. This time, however, change the ending. How would you finish the story if you were the author?

2. In pairs, write a dialogue in which one of you is Henry, the border guard, and the other is the factory worker. Decide on what you will say to each other as you meet at the frontier to undergo the daily examination

of the factory worker before allowing him to cross the border. Be sure to include mention of your suspicion as the border guard.

3. The factory worker had succeeded in smuggling many bicycles across the border before he revealed his secret. Is there some secret activity that you or someone you know is engaged in? Describe the activity, giving all the details, so that we can appreciate your ability to function as a spy. Of course, you realize that this question is designed to ask you to be as creative as you can. There is absolutely no need to be truthful.

4. Border guards are an important part of a country's defense system. People should not be allowed to move freely across borders and go from one country to another. This kind of movement of populations might cause great world disturbances.

Do you agree or disagree?

Write an essay the very best way you can. Use your knowledge of the world, what you have read, and/or what you have studied to support your point of view.

5. Please choose your own topic and write about it.

Exercise 10.
DICTATION

Directions:

Your teacher will dictate the following sentences to you. Your job is to write them as accurately as you can. As you write your sentences, remember to use correct spelling and punctuation. Finally, even if you don't hear every word clearly, try to use all the clues in the sentence to help you figure out the difficult word. Do what you have practiced in the doing of the cloze.

1. Henry used to work as a border guard.
2. He made sure that people didn't smuggle anything.
3. He used to inspect the bundles they carried.
4. He used to be very suspicious.
5. Therefore, he used to examine the bundles very carefully.
6. The factory worker crossed the border every day.

7. Henry did not work on Saturday and Sunday.
8. The worker took a new bicycle over the border every day.
9. The factory worker was a very clever man.
10. Henry was not a very good border guard.

Unit 8
WORDS AND THEIR MEANINGS

Exercise 1.
MAKING PREDICTIONS (DRTA)

Directions:

Read the title of the cloze that your teacher has written on the board. Based on the information that you see on the board, see how many predictions you can make about the story that you are about to read.

We are going to complete this sentence:

We're going to find out . . .

Example:

1. We're going to find out about some special meanings of words.

Now you and your peers will think of additional predictions as one of your classmates writes them on the board.

_____

_____

_____

_____

_____

_____

_____

_____

_____

_____

_____

_____

_____

_____

_____

_____

_____

_____

Exercise 2.
DOING THE CLOZE

Directions:

Read the entire passage to yourself first. Do not try to fill the blanks before you have completed reading the story. When you have finished reading, you are ready to start working with the other members of your group to fill the blanks. Together, you are going to decide on appropriate fillers for each of the blanks.

There are three rules that you need to remember:

Rule 1.   You can use only *one* word to fill the blank.
Rule 2.   The word must make sense both to the sentence it is in and to the entire story.
Rule 3.   The word you choose must be grammatically correct and spelled correctly.

Note: In the letter to the student, you read that you will need to think about what you are doing. Here is your opportunity to show what you already know about English.

WORDS AND THEIR MEANINGS

Ms. Williams lived in _____ village. She used to _____
(1) (2)
to the beach with _____ husband and her children _____
(3) (4)
year on vacation, but _____ had never been abroad.
(5)
_____ Ms. Williams's village there _____
(6) (7)
a women's club, which _____ meetings every week. Ms.
(8)
_____ enjoyed these meetings very _____.
(9) (10)
Each year the Women's _____ arranged a trip to _____
(11) (12)
or Spain or Italy _____ those members who wanted _____
(13) (14)
go. They used to _____ in a big bus _____
(15) (16)
stay in small hotels, _____ the trip was inexpensive. _____
(17) (18)
Ms. Williams was not _____ to go because she _____
(19) (20)
to take care of _____ children.
(21)
Then the year _____ when Ms. Williams's children
(22)
_____ all adults, and she _____ not have to take
(23) (24)
_____ of them any more. _____ Williams's husband said to
(25) (26)
_____, "Daisy, if you want _____ go abroad this summer
(27) (28)
_____ your friends, please go. _____ can look after myself
(29) (30)
_____ two weeks."
(31)
Ms. Williams _____ very glad. She went _____
(32) (33)
Spanish classes in the _____ every week to learn _____
(34) (35)
little Spanish for her _____. Finally, when July 15th _____
(36) (37)
and she got into _____ bus to start her _____
(38) (39)
vacation abroad, she knew _____ useful words of that
(40)
_____.
(41)
One evening, when the _____ had stopped for the _____
(42) (43)
in a small Spanish _____, Ms. Williams and two _____
(44) (45)
her best friends decided _____ go for a walk. _____
(46) (47)

came to a place _____ (48) few strangers went, and _____ (49)
several women and children _____ (50) round them and began
_____ (51) whisper to each other _____ (52) the foreigners. Ms.
Williams _____ (53) a word that she _____ (54).

   "Oh, no," she said _____ (55) them in her kindest _____ (56).
"We're not foreigners. We're _____ (57). You're foreigners."

Exercise 3.
EXAMINING THE FILLERS FOR THE CLOZE

Directions:

Look at the choices you have made for the blanks in your text as each
person reads a sentence with the fillers he or she has chosen for the
blanks. If your choice differs from the one you hear, and you are not sure
if your answer is correct, ask your teacher to explain. Often there is more
than one appropriate filler for the blank. Check to see whether you have
spelled the word correctly and whether you have put the capital letters,
periods, and other punctuation marks where they belong.

Exercise 4.
EXAMINATION OF PREDICTIONS

Directions:

As you and your class go over each prediction that you made earlier, you
are going to decide whether the statement is *implicit, explicit,* or *unknown,* based on the story you have just read. Be sure to ask your teacher
if these words are not clear to you. As you read each prediction, think
about what you have read in the story and then decide. It will often be
necessary to go back to the text and find justification for your answer.

Exercise 5.
READER RESPONSE SHEET

Directions:

Please answer the following questions in complete sentences.

Example:

   1. What do we call stories that carry a moral message?
      We call stories that carry a moral message fables.

2. Do you think the author of this story succeeded in presenting us with a moral message? Why? Why not?

_____

_____

_____

_____

_____

3. Did you like the story? Why? Why not?

_____

_____

_____

_____

4. Do you think you would like to meet Ms. Williams? Why? Why not?

_____

_____

_____

_____

5. Do you think that having women's clubs is a good idea? Why? Why not?

_____

_____

_____

_____

6. Do you think that if a busload of tourists came to your neighborhood, people would be interested in them? Why? Why not?

_____

_____

_____

_____

_____

7. Do you think that if a busload of tourists had come to your neighborhood in your country, your neighbors might have been interested in them? Why? Why not?

_____

_____

_____

_____

_____

8. What are some questions that you have about the story?

_____

_____

_____

_____

_____

_____

_____

_____

_____

9. What vocabulary words and/or expressions are not clear to you?

_____   _____   _____

_____   _____   _____

_____   _____   _____

10. What two things did you learn from doing this cloze, and how are you going to practice them? Please be specific.

_____

_____

_____

_____

_____

_____

Exercise 6.
COMPREHENSION/DISCUSSION QUESTIONS

Directions:

Please read the following questions. Discuss them with your peers, and then write the answers in complete sentences.

Example:

1. What kind of women belong to a women's club in a small town?
   All kinds of women belong to a women's club in a small town.

2. Why do you think they belong to a club?

_____

_____

_____

_____

3. Do you think it is fair that Ms. Williams had not been able to go on vacation with her friends until her children were grown? Why? Why not?

_____

_____

_____

_____

_____

_____

_____

4. How would you have spent your vacation if you had been Ms. Williams?

_____

_____

_____

_____

_____

5. How did Ms. Williams prepare for her vacation? What does that tell us about her?

_____

_____

_____

_____

_____

6. Why do you think Ms. Williams waited for her husband to suggest that she go on vacation with her friends? What does that tell us about this couple?

_____

_____

_____

_____

_____

7. Do you think women in your country would have had a life similar to Ms. Williams's? Why? Why not?

_____

_____

_____

_____

_____

_____

8. Why did the women and children gather round Ms. Williams and her friends?

_____

_____

_____

_____

9. What do you think of Ms. Williams's response to the Spanish people when she understood what they were saying? How might you have responded to them?

_____

_____

_____

_____

_____

10. Has anybody ever called you a foreigner? How do you feel about being a newcomer to this country?

_____

_____

_____

_____

_____

_____

Exercise 7.
GRAMMAR POINT

Direct Quotations

Often it is necessary to include in our writing exactly what somebody says. For example:

1. Ms. Williams said, "We are going to the beach."
2. Mr. Williams said, "Daisy, you can go on vacation."
3. The pilot said, "The weather is fine."

These sentences indicate that the writer is reporting exactly what somebody said. These kinds of sentences are called *direct quotations* because we write the exact words that somebody has spoken.

Form:

A direct quotation has *quotation marks (" ")* around the words that the person spoke. A direct quotation also starts with a capital letter. There is a comma immediately before the quotation marks. When we mention the person to whom we are speaking, we add a comma after the person's name, as in sentence 2. Furthermore, we can indicate the speaker either at the beginning or at the end of the sentence, as follows:

> Mr. Williams said, "Daisy, go on vacation if you like."
> Mr. Williams said, "Go on vacation if you like, Daisy."

Directions:

Think about some statements that people in the story might have said to each other. For example:

> Ms. Williams said to her children, "I am going to Spain."

See whether you can make up five sentences from the story. Think about your first days in the United States or think of a vacation you took. Choose a partner and write a dialogue using one of those situations.

_____

_____

_____

_____

_____

_____

_____

_____

_____

_____

_____

_____

_____

Exercise 8.
WORD BUILDING

Two-word Verbs

We have just read about Ms. Williams who could not *take off* on vacation because she had to *take care of* her children. Because her children were young, Ms. Williams had to *give up* her vacation with her friends. Instead, she and her husband *took* the children *along* when they went to the beach each summer.

The italicized verbs above are called two-word verbs (in one case, three-word verb). These verbs are made up of a main verb plus a particle or little word. The particle may be a preposition like *up* or *of* or an adverb like *along*. In either case, we need to use both parts of the two-part verb, otherwise we will not be able to express the meaning we have in mind. For example, if we take the word *get* and add to it the particle *up,* we have *get up*.

We *get up* every morning. (We awaken from our sleep.)

When we add *down* to *get,* we get *get down*.

The women *got down from* the bus.

When we add *into* to *get,* we get *get into*.

The women *got into* the bus.

When we add *through* to *get,* we get *get through*.

I'm so tired; I hope I can *get through* the day.

You can see that each of these meanings is very different from the others. How will you learn them? BY MEMORIZING. There are a number of frequently used two-word verbs, some of which you may already know. We are going to work on several of them and see whether we can memorize them easily. We have already worked with one important verb — *get*. Here are some others:

be	catch	fall	keep	run
break	come	figure	let	sit
bring	cut	fill	look	stand
call	do	go	make	take
carry	draw	hold	pick	talk
			put	turn

The following are some commonly used particles:

about	at	down	of	over
across	away	for	off	through
along	back	in	on	to
around	by	into	out	up
				with

Use your dictionary to help you find the meanings of these two-word verbs. Then we will be ready to start using them in sentences.

Example:

Ms. Williams could not *take off* on vacation with her friends. She and her husband were busy *bringing up* their children. Ms. Williams had to wait until her children could *take care of* themselves. Then she was able to *catch up* on the vacation she had missed.

Directions:

Choose a verb and a particle from the two lists above. Write about ten sentences. See how many of the two-word verb combinations you can use. If you can, write a paragraph using these two-word verb combinations. Perhaps you could use the word *get* in several different ways. Don't forget to use your dictionary to help you with the meanings.

_____

_____

_____

_____

_____

_____

_____

_____

In addition to learning the meaning of each of these two-word verbs, we also need to remember another important fact. Sometimes we can shift the particle and put it before or after the complement. For example, we can shift the particle *up* and put it before or after the complement *Tom* as in the following sentences:

> I'll *call* Tom *up*.
> I'll *call up* Tom.

But, when we want to use the pronoun *him* instead of the noun *Tom*, we no longer have that option.

> We can only say: I'll *call* him *up*.
> We cannot say: I'll *call* + *up* + him.

The rule is that when the complement is a pronoun, that pronoun *always* comes *between* the two parts of the two-part verb.

> They'll take *them* along on vacation.

A second fact that we need to remember about these two-word verbs is that some of these verbs can be separated, while others cannot.

> We can say: The child *ran after* the ball.
> We cannot say: The child ran the ball after.

How do we know which two-word verbs are separable and which are unseparable? The answer is that we don't know. The truth is that we need to pay close attention to how these particular verbs are used in English. They are important because they are used a great deal by speakers and writers of English and not knowing them may seriously interfere with our ability to function in English. So, although it seems almost impossible to learn these verbs, it really isn't. Here are two hints that you may find useful.

1. Don't use a pronoun if you're not sure whether the verb is separable or unseparable.

> I'll *look him up* when I visit New York. (That's fine.)
> I'll *look up him* when I visit New York. (This is incorrect.)

2. Test your combination by putting a noun after the two-word verb. Often you will immediately recognize that that combination does not go in English. Most of all, learn to be a good language detective and watch how other people use these two-word combinations.

Here are some examples:

The son *will carry on* the father's work.

The son *will carry* the father's work *on*. (This does not work.)

She *took up* tennis.

She *took* tennis *up*. (This does not work.)

Directions:

Choose some two-word combinations from the list on page 122 and write a paragraph about anything that interests you.

_____

_____

_____

_____

_____

_____

_____

_____

Exercise 9.
WRITING ACTIVITIES

Directions:

Please read the following suggested topics. Then choose one topic and write about it.

1. Write a summary of the story of Ms. Williams. Although you are free to use your imagination, please be sure to include all the necessary facts in your story.

2. Choose a partner or two and write a dialogue in which you describe a conversation between Ms. Williams and her friends. Ms. Williams's children are still too young for her to leave them. However, her friends are

trying to persuade Ms. Williams to go to Italy with the Women's Club anyway.

Or: Write a dialogue describing what happened to Ms. Williams and her two friends after she explained to the Spanish people that they were British and that the Spaniards were the foreigners.

3. When we go abroad, we should know the language of the country we are visiting. Write about the advantages and disadvantages to visitors of knowing the language of the country they visit.

4. Knowing more than one language is advantageous. People who are bilingual enjoy a richer, fuller life and have access to two different cultures.

Do you agree or disagree?

Write an essay the very best way you can. Use your knowledge of the world, what you have read, and/or what you have studied to support your point of view.

5. Please choose your own topic and write about it.

Exercise 10.
DICTATION

Directions:

Your teacher will dictate the following sentences to you. Your job is to write them as accurately as you can. As you write your sentences, remember to use correct spelling and punctuation. Finally, even if you don't hear every word clearly, try to use all the clues in the sentence to help you figure out the difficult word. Do what you have practiced in the doing of the cloze.

1. Ms. Williams was a member of the Women's Club in her small town.
2. The Women's Club went on vacation each year without Ms. Williams.
3. She took care of her children until they grew up.
4. Ms. Williams could then think about a vacation abroad.
5. Mr. Williams said, "Daisy, go on vacation with your club."
6. Ms. Williams planned to go to Spain with her friends.
7. She studied Spanish and was prepared for her trip abroad.
8. The bus stopped for the night in a small Spanish town.
9. The Spanish women and children talked about the foreigners.
10. Ms. Williams said, "We are not foreigners."

Unit 9
A CREATIVE PAINTER

Exercise 1.
MAKING PREDICTIONS (DRTA)

Directions:

Read the title of the cloze that your teacher has written on the board. Based on the information that you see on the board, see how many predictions you can make about the story that you are about to read.

We are going to complete this sentence:

We're going to find out . . .

Example:

1. We're going to find out why the painter is creative.

Now you and your peers will think of additional predictions as one of your classmates writes them on the board.

_____

_____

_____

_____

_____

_____

_____

_____

_____

_____

_____

_____

_____

_____

_____

Exercise 2.
DOING THE CLOZE

Directions:

Read the entire passage to yourself first. Do not try to fill the blanks before you have completed reading the story. When you have finished reading, you are ready to start working with the other members of your group to fill the blanks. Together, you are going to decide on appropriate fillers for each of the blanks.

There are three rules that you need to remember:

Rule 1.   You can use only _one_ word to fill the blank.
Rule 2.   The word must make sense both to the sentence it is in and to the entire story.
Rule 3.   The word you choose must be grammatically correct and spelled correctly.

Note: In the letter to the student, you read that you will need to think about what you are doing. Here is your opportunity to show what you already know about English.

A CREATIVE PAINTER

Ms. Miller lived alone _____ a small house. She _____
(1)   (2)
beautiful things and had _____ her curtains, her carpets,
(3)
_____ her furniture so well _____ everybody who visited her
(4)   (5)
_____ always said, "How beautifully _____
(6)   (7)
have arranged everything!"

But _____ walls in Ms. Miller's _____
(8)   (9)
were beginning to get _____ little dirty, so she _____
(10)   (11)
to have the room _____ again. She waited until _____
(12)   (13)
summer because she wanted _____ spend a week at _____
(14)   (15)
beach then, and she _____ that it would be _____
(16)   (17)
if the room was _____ while she was away.
(18)

_____ she left for her _____, she called a painter
(19)   (20)
_____, showed him a purple _____, which she liked very
(21)   (22)
_____, and asked him to _____ the bedroom exactly the
(23)   (24)
_____ color. She told him _____ she would be away
(25)   (26)
_____ a week, and that _____ wanted the work to
(27)   (28)
_____ finished before she came _____.
(29)   (30)

For three days the _____ mixed purple paint and _____
(31)   (32)
paint and red paint _____ white paint together, but _____
(33)   (34)
was not able to _____ exactly the same color. _____
(35)   (36)
when Ms. Miller came _____, the bedroom and the _____
(37)   (38)
were exactly the same _____. She looked at the _____
(39)   (40)
walls and then at _____ ashtray and felt very _____.
(41)   (42)

Several evenings later the _____ was having a drink
(43)
_____ a friend. The friend _____ him whether it was
(44)   (45)
_____ difficult to please the _____ for whom he worked.
(46)   (47)
_____ the painter told him _____ story of Ms. Miller.
(48)   (49)

" _____ you know," he said, " _____ a very strange
  (50)   (51)

thing, _____ she still hasn't realized _____ I painted her
         (52)   (53)

ashtray _____ the same paint that _____ used for her
          (54)   (55)

walls."

Exercise 3.
EXAMINING THE FILLERS FOR THE CLOZE

Directions:

Look at the choices you have made for the blanks in your text as each
person reads a sentence with the fillers he or she has chosen for the
blanks. If your choice differs from the one you hear, and you are not sure
if your answer is correct, ask your teacher to explain. Often there is more
than one appropriate filler for the blank. Check to see whether you have
spelled the word correctly and whether you have put the capital letters,
periods, and other punctuation marks where they belong.

Exercise 4.
EXAMINATION OF PREDICTIONS

Directions:

As you and your class go over each prediction that you made earlier, you
are going to decide whether the statement is *implicit, explicit,* or *unknown,* based on the story you have just read. Be sure to ask your teacher
if these words are not clear to you. As you read each prediction, think
about what you have read in the story and then decide. It will often be
necessary to go back to the text and find justification for your answer.

Exercise 5.
READER RESPONSE SHEET

Directions:

Please answer the following questions in complete sentences.

Example:

1. Why do you think the author wrote the story?
   The author wrote the story to tell us about a creative painter.

2. Do you think the author was successful in achieving that aim? Why? Why not?

_____

_____

_____

_____

3. What are some questions that you have about the story?

Example:

Why did the painter work so hard to match the color of the ashtray?

_____

_____

_____

_____

_____

_____

_____

4. What are some words that are not clear to you? (Have you examined the context carefully to see whether you can decide the meanings?)

_____   _____   _____

_____   _____   _____

5. What two things did you learn from doing the cloze, and how are you going to practice them? Please be specific.

_____

_____

_____

_____

_____

_____

Exercise 6.
COMPREHENSION/DISCUSSION QUESTIONS

Directions:

Please read the following questions. Discuss them with your peers, and then write the answers in complete sentences.

Example:

1. Why did people often compliment Ms. Miller on her home?
   People often complimented Mrs. Miller because she had arranged her home beautifully.

2. Why did she decide to have her bedroom painted while she was on vacation?

   _____

   _____

   _____

3. Why did Ms. Miller choose to show the painter the purple ashtray rather than simply tell him that she wanted her walls painted purple?

   _____

   _____

   _____

4. How did the painter try to match the color of the ashtray with his paint?

   _____

   _____

   _____

5. Why was it difficult for him to match the purple color of the ashtray? Have you ever tried to match colors? What happened?

   _____

   _____

   _____

   _____

6. In your opinion, did he try hard enough to find the exact color? Why?
   Why not?

   _____

   _____

   _____

7. How did the painter finally solve his problem?

   _____

   _____

   _____

8. What do you think of the solution?

   _____

   _____

   _____

9. Although Ms. Miller was very careful about all her possessions, she
   did not notice what the painter had done? Why?

   _____

   _____

   _____

10. Would you hire the painter to have your apartment painted? Why?
    Why not?

    _____

    _____

    _____

Exercise 7.
GRAMMAR POINT

To Have + Complement

   A. In English, we use this structure to explain that we are asking or
hiring someone to do something for us, as Ms. Miller did when she hired

the painter *to have her bedroom painted.* (You may remember that in the first story, "How to Have Your Hair Cut," we read about a man who managed to have his hair cut without paying.)

Form:

Ms. Miller   wanted   to have   her bedroom   painted.
   S   +   V   + to have +   something   + past participle

  The man   managed   to have   his hair   cut.
     S   +   V   + to have + something + past participle

Directions:

Write five things that you would like to have done without doing them yourself.

Example:

1. I wanted to have the house cleaned.

_____

_____

_____

_____

_____

_____

    B. When we mention the person we want to do something for us, we use a slightly different structure.

Form:

Ms. Miller   wants   to have   the painter   paint   the bedroom.
  S   +   V   + to have +   someone   + base form +   complement
  S   +   V   + to have +   someone   +   do   +   something

The student   wanted   to have   the teacher   write   the essay.
   S   +   V   + to have +   someone   + do + something

Directions:

Think about some things you wanted, decided, or would like to have done and write five sentences using the form you have just learned.

Note: There is a difference between the two structures.

1. Ms. Miller wanted to have the bedroom painted.
2. Ms. Miller wanted to have the painter paint the bedroom.

_____

_____

_____

_____

_____

_____

_____

_____

_____

There are two other verbs in English that behave the same way as the verb *to have* above. They are *to let* and *to make*.

Examples:

Ms. Miller	let	the painter	paint	her room.
S	+ V +	someone	+ base form +	complement
S	+ V +	someone	+ do +	something

The lifeguard	made	the swimmers	wear	bathing caps.
S	+ V +	someone	+ do +	something

Directions:

Now write five examples of these patterns.

_____

_____

_____

_____

_____

_____

_____

_____

_____

_____

_____

Exercise 8.
WORD BUILDING

Adjectives

In this story, we read about a creative painter and a fastidious home-maker. You know what *creative* means. What do you think *fastidious* means? What clues in the story helped you to find the meaning of *fastidious*?

There are other words that we can use to describe the painter and Ms. Miller. Words that are used to describe or give us more information about nouns are called *adjectives*. In the title "A Creative Painter," the word *creative* is an adjective.

In English, the adjective usually comes before the noun, and we do not show number — singular or plural — in an adjective. So we say:

> The good girl.
> The good girls.

Neither do we show whether the adjective is male or female, as is often done in other languages. We say:

> The good girl.
> The good boy.

Directions:

Think about the painter and Ms. Miller. What words could you use to describe each of them? For example, in addition to being creative, what else could we say about the painter? Similarly, in addition to fastidious, what words could we use to describe Ms. Miller? Make a list of ten adjectives, five for the painter and five for Ms. Miller. Then write a summary of the story; use as many of the adjectives that you have on your list as possible.

Ms. Miller   **The Painter**

_____   _____

_____   _____

_____   _____

_____   _____

_____   _____

Now write a summary of the story.

_____

_____

_____

_____

_____

_____

_____

_____

_____

_____

_____

Think about the effect of these added words, adjectives, on the story. Do they add to the story? How? You probably realize that these words are of great significance in writing, and you may want to include these kinds of words in your own future writing.

Exercise 9.
WRITING ACTIVITIES

Directions:

Please read the following suggested topics. Then choose one and write about it.

1. Write a dialogue in which Ms. Miller is talking to the painter. She is explaining that she wants to have the bedroom painted. She is going to have the work done while she is on vacation. Include in your dialogue all the arrangements for that painting (or other work) that Ms. Miller would like to have done.

2. Because having her house painted was unpleasant, Ms. Miller chose to go on vacation.

   Think about an unpleasant situation in your life. You are really having difficulty confronting that situation, and you are looking for some alternatives.

   Write a paper in which you explain the situation facing you and the arrangements you have made to make that unpleasant situation better. Include all the necessary details so that the reader can fully appreciate your situation.

3. There are some people who might say the painter deceived Ms. Miller and that he really lied to her. Others might not agree. They argue that sometimes we need to tell a "little white lie" in order to get along in this world.

   Do you agree or disagree?

   Write an essay the very best way you can. Use your knowledge of the world, what you have read, and/or what you have studied to support your point of view.

4. Write a dialogue in which you, the painter, explain to someone else how you solved the problem with your customer, Ms. Miller. Include in this dialogue your general ideas on how to satisfy your customers so that you can run a successful business. You might talk to a therapist friend of yours or a trusted teacher or adviser who would like to use that kind of information in a human relations course.

5. Please choose your own topic and write your essay.

Exercise 10.
DICTATION

Directions:

Your teacher will dictate the following sentences to you. Your job is to write them as accurately as you can. As you write your sentences, remember to use correct spelling and punctuation. Finally, even if you don't hear every word clearly, try to use all the clues in the sentence to help you figure out the difficult word. Do what you have practiced in doing the cloze.

1. Ms. Miller took good care of everything in her house.
2. All her visitors admired her beautiful things.
3. She decided to have her dirty walls painted.
4. She had the painter match the walls to her pretty ashtray.
5. Meanwhile, Ms. Miller went on her summer vacation.
6. The painter tried hard to match the walls to the ashtray.
7. He mixed the paint again and again to get the exact color.
8. He couldn't find the exact color, but he had a good idea.
9. He painted the walls and the ashtray the same color.
10. Ms. Miller didn't notice that he had changed the color.

ADDITIONAL CLOZES

PLASTIC: A FRIEND TURNED ENEMY

Directions:

Please read the entire passage first. Then go back and fill each space with *one* appropriate word. Be sure that the word is spelled correctly, is grammatically correct, and makes sense to the whole story as well as to the sentence in which it appears.

Plastic is a material widely produced during World War II to compensate for the shortage of materials during that world conflict. Today, about 45 years later, that plastic, which had been invented to aid humanity at a critical time in world history, now threatens nature itself.

A number of scientists believe that _____ is the most far-
                                      (1)
reaching, man-made threat _____ many marine species today.
                           (2)
Plastic annually _____ or cripples tens of thousands of _____,
                  (3)   (4)
seabirds, sea lions, and sea otters, _____ hundreds of whales,
                                      (5)
dolphins, porpoises, and _____ turtles. Plastic behaves differently
                          (6)
from oil _____ or toxic chemical spills. Both those _____ are
          (7)   (8)

concentrated in one place. But ____(9)____ behave like mines; they float
around ____(10)____ ocean waiting for a victim.

The ____(11)____ first learned of plastic's devastating effect
____(12)____ an entire population of marine animals _____
____(13)____ the late 1970s. The first victims ____(14)____ the northern
seals of the Pribilof ____(15)____ located in the Bering Sea near
____(16)____. Beginning in 1976, scientists noticed that _____
____(17)____ seal population was decreasing rapidly each ____(18)____.
After some careful observations, the scientists ____(19)____
that plastic entanglement was killing up ____(20)____
40,000 seals a year.

This is ____(21)____ the plastic kills. Because seals are _____
____(22)____ curious, they play with fragments of ____(23)____ netting or packing
straps floating on ____(24)____ water. They often catch their necks
____(25)____ the webbing, reported Dr. Fowler, a ____(26)____ who
visits the islands every summer. ____(27)____ debris constricts the seals'
movements, preventing ____(28)____ animals from feeding normally.
The animals ____(29)____ then unable to pull themselves away
____(30)____ the debris. They eventually drown, starve ____(31)____
death, or die of infection or ____(32)____ from deep wounds caused by
their ____(33)____ to free themselves from the plastic.

____(34)____ problem is not with the plastics ____(35)____
but in the way people dispose ____(36)____ them. Until only recently, no
laws ____(37)____ specifically prohibited ocean disposal and dumping
____(38)____ plastics. As a result, ships have ____(39)____ the ocean
their dumping grounds, getting ____(40)____ of waste in a careless
manner. ____(41)____ is today the favored American material —
____(42)____, lightweight, safer than glass, and less ____(43)____ than
leather. Because it is so ____(44)____ and resistant to destruction, it

floats _____ the surface of the water, and _____ animals
(45)   (46)
often mistake it for food. _____ addition, plastic is often
(47)
transparent and _____ animals that cannot see it. It _____
(48)   (49)
the most common type of sea _____ today. Thus, plastic,
(50)
invented to improve _____ life, is an unexpected factor in
(51)
_____ pollution and death to marine life.
(52)

EDUCATION FOR DEMOCRACY: A POTENTIAL AMERICAN EXPORT

Directions:

Please read the entire passage first. Then go back and fill each space with
one appropriate word. Be sure that the word is spelled correctly, is grammatically correct, and makes sense to the whole story as well as to the
sentence in which it appears.

Eastern Europe has begun to revolt against the oppression of
communism. In Central and South America, people in country after
country are also demanding a free and democratic society. The question
then arises: How can the young be educated to live in a democracy
when their elders never experienced that form of government? The
Child Development Project in California, as well as some creative
educational experiments nationwide, may put the United States in a
position to export the how's of democracy along with the many
consumer goods this country has to offer the world.

The Child Development Project involves 3,000 _____
(1)
in seven elementary schools in California. _____
(2)
schools lie east and south of _____ Francisco and include
(3)
children from a _____ of socioeconomic backgrounds.
(4)

Although educators have _____ (5) believed that classroom

management techniques must _____ (6) on a system of rewards and

(7) _____, this project has taken a new _____ (8)

to education for democracy. The goal _____ (9)

for children to become self-controlled. That _____ (10),

children themselves must set the standards _____ (11)

good behavior and monitor themselves as _____ (12).

Discipline is used as a way _____ (13) promote altruistic values

and cooperative behavior _____ (14) children. Discipline

is considered a long-range _____ (15) in this project and not an

(16) _____ response to some action. In short, _____ (17)

become both independent and interdependent by _____ (18)

to function on their own and _____ (19) a group.

Thus, the approach of _____ (20) educators

includes efforts to enhance the _____ (21) social and moral

development as well _____ (22) their cognitive development. Teachers

help students _____ (23) how to live in a democracy _____ (24)

behaving democratically. For example, children learn _____ (25)

respect each other's ideas, they learn _____ (26) listen to each other

and to _____ (27), and they set standards and understand the

(28) _____ for standards and reasons why rules _____ (29) behavior

are needed.

Moreover, these educators _____ (30) that the essence of classroom

discipline _____ (31) in teachers' developing positive relationships

with _____ (32) students. Teachers try to explain, not _____ (33);

therefore, they speak privately to those _____ (34) who misbehave.

When children are sent _____ (35) of the room for misbehaving, the

(36) _____ themselves decide when they are ready _____ (37) return

to the group. Finally, students _____ (38) in groups to practice "social

goals" _____ as learning to listen to their _____, helping
(39)   (40)

each other, and learning to _____ ideas or opinions different from
(41)

theirs.

_____ is clear that those countries striving _____
(42)   (43)

a democratic way of life need _____ than consumer goods from
(44)

the United _____. They also need to know how _____
(45)   (46)

educate their young in preparation for _____ new life. The
(47)

California project is _____ example of American educators'
(48)

continuous efforts _____ prepare youth for life in a _____.
(49)   (50)

Other efforts in collaborative learning have _____ shown
(51)

remarkable success. Perhaps we need _____ export some of these
(52)

educational ideas _____ those countries just starting to walk
(53)

_____ road to democracy.
(54)

SPACE: THE SILENT COMMUNICATOR

Directions:

Please read the entire passage first. Then go back and fill each space with
one appropriate word. Be sure that the word is spelled correctly, is grammatically correct, and makes sense to the whole story as well as to the
sentence in which it appears.

Several factors impact on the way we use space to communicate. For
the most part, our use of space is determined by our personality and the
culture in which we grew up. Although we are usually not aware of our
feelings about space in particular situations, any violation by others of
what we know to be the appropriate use of space may make us
uncomfortable.

We use space to communicate with _____ another.
(1)

The distance between us and _____ (2) else may
determine the nature of _____ (3) communication. If we are a few
_____ (4) away from someone's ear, we will _____ (5) whisper,
and the nature of the _____ (6) will be secret. An even greater
_____ (7) in tone and kind of message _____ (8)
when we speak to a large _____ (9). Here the nature of the message
_____ (10) be determined in part by the _____ (11)
between us and the most distant _____ (12) of the audience.

   Space "speaks" also _____ (13) the way that we distribute
ourselves _____ (14) a classroom, bus, or lecture hall. _____ (15)
free to choose, most people will _____ (16)
to sit as far from strangers _____ (17) possible. The distance they
select to _____ (18) themselves from others in the audience,
_____ (19) from the speaker, is in itself _____ (20) form of
communication. In regimented institutions, _____ (21) as the military
service, the distance _____ (22) be maintained between persons of
different _____ (23) may be regulated.

   The private space _____ (24) each of us has is sometimes
_____ (25) "territoriality." It is as if we _____ (26) around with a
plastic bubble hovering _____ (27) us. When this space is violated,
_____ (28) when someone gets too close, we _____ (29) become
tense or even hostile, and _____ (30) will affect the nature of the
_____ (31). Most Americans and Englishmen prefer a _____ (32)
distance for normal discourse. They feel _____ (33) comfortable if a
certain space between _____ (34) and the other person is maintained.
_____ (35) the other hand, people of Latin _____ (36) descent
apparently prefer a smaller distance. _____ (37) is not hard to imagine
a _____ (38) in which a Latin American talks _____ (39) a North
American and the North _____ (40) keeps retreating to maintain what

she _____ he considers an appropriate distance.
(41)

However, _____ are times when we must sacrifice _____
(42)   (43)
feeling of comfort for the advantage _____ getting someplace.
(44)
For example, in a _____ subway or bus, we allow others
(45)
_____ get closer to us than we _____ would because we
(46)   (47)
have a goal _____ mind, which is to get to _____ particular
(48)   (49)
destination. The person near us _____ giving up his or her private
(50)
space _____ the very same reason. Civilized behavior
(51)
_____ demands that we be careful not _____ intrude on
(52)   (53)
others more than is _____ by crowding too close.
(54)

As the _____ becomes smaller through extensive travel and
(55)
_____ movement of people from one country _____
(56)   (57)
another, we need to remember that _____
(58)
is a silent, but significant, communicator. _____
(59)
of the space of others may _____ done unconsciously;
(60)
awareness of variations of _____
(61)
views of space individually and culturally _____
(62)
help to prevent some of these _____.
(63)

Appendix
PAST FORMS OF
IRREGULAR VERBS

Present	Past
be	was, were
become	became
begin	began
blow	blew
break	broke
bring	brought
buy	bought
catch	caught
come	came
cost	cost
cut	cut
do	did
drink	drank
drive	drove
eat	ate
fall	fell
feel	felt
fight	fought
find	found
fly	flew
forget	forgot

Present	Past
get	got
give	gave
go	went
grow	grew
have	had
hear	heard
hold	held
hurt	hurt
keep	kept
know	knew
leave	left
lend	lent
lose	lost
make	made
mean	meant
meet	met
pay	paid
put	put
read	read
ride	rode
ring	rang
run	ran
say	said
see	saw
sell	sold
send	sent
shut	shut
sing	sang
sit	sat
sleep	slept
speak	spoke
spend	spent
stand	stood
steal	stole
sweep	swept
take	took
teach	taught
tell	told
think	thought

Present	**Past**
throw	threw
understand	understood
wear	wore
win	won
write	wrote

ANSWER KEY

Unit 1.
HOW TO HAVE YOUR HAIR CUT

1. barbershop
2. of
3. of
4. The
5. hurry, rush
6. barber, proprietor
7. first
8. hair
9. the
10. boy
11. barber
12. When
13. man
14. chair
15. in
16. dresses, excuses
17. he
18. hurry, rush
19. barber
20. cut
21. he
22. a
23. for
24. and
25. to
26. The
27. boy's, child's
28. up
29. the
30. to
31. passes
32. barber
33. Don't
34. be
35. But
36. the

37. playing, skating
38. he
39. Come

40. boy
41. barbershop
42. hair

Unit 2.
PEOPLE'S BEST FRIEND

1. and
2. tell, hear, read
3. is
4. a
5. Seeing
6. special, particular
7. people, men, women
8. and
9. We, People, Trainers
10. dogs
11. the
12. people, men, women
13. to
14. go
15. several, some
16. to
17. day, morning, afternoon
18. and
19. got
20. The
21. people
22. seats
23. stood, got
24. seat, place
25. old, blind
26. but

27. room, space
28. push, nudge
29. side
30. He
31. the
32. then
33. for
34. blind, old
35. the
36. the
37. of
38. sat
39. and
40. the
41. man
42. and
43. in, on
44. smile, grin
45. the
46. for
47. at
48. a, some
49. it
50. off
51. got
52. master, owner

Unit 3.
THE OBSERVANT STUDENTS AND
THEIR CLEVER PROFESSOR

1. want, wish, like
2. But
3. that
4. the
5. him
6. go
7. cut
8. that
9. with
10. weeks
11. and
12. one
13. very, quite
14. time, months
15. bet
16. his
17. barber
18. long
19. a
20. of
21. a, the
22. classroom, office
23. bet
24. dollar
25. write, put, scribble
26. date
27. the
28. student, person, man, woman
29. date
30. visit, trip
31. all
32. jar
33. puzzled, confused
34. paper, list
35. table, scene
36. for
37. for
38. and
39. he, Jones
40. and
41. math, logic, philosophy
42. jot, note, write
43. which
44. list, paper
45. to
46. a
47. realized
48. he, Jones
49. he
50. put, stuffed
51. jar
52. the, that
53. paper
54. and
55. collect, take
56. that

Unit 4.
AN UNDISCIPLINED SOLDIER

1. hot, warm
2. sitting, seated
3. very
4. soldier
5. army, military, training
6. and, where
7. soldier, unit
8. and
9. had, needed, planned
10. the
11. whole, entire, complete
12. sun
13. real
14. soldiers, guys
15. whose
16. always, often, frequently
17. his
18. never, not
19. the
20. particular, certain, hot
21. a
22. I'll
23. I
24. desert, field, sun
25. pretend, train
26. So, Therefore
27. go
28. the
29. tall, large, old, gigantic
30. the
31. one
32. waited, hid
33. Then
34. the
35. read, examine, peruse
36. brought, taken
37. when
38. the
39. quickly, quietly
40. He
41. on
42. so
43. as
44. who, that
45. day
46. When
47. camp, base
48. began, started
49. the
50. had, all
51. If
52. real, live, true
53. all
54. dead, finished, gone
55. shouted, called
56. that
57. he
58. that
59. punished
60. Robinson
61. charge, command
62. soldier, one
63. see

Unit 5.
THE APPROPRIATENESS OF KNOWLEDGE

1. lecturer, professor
2. knew, spoke, read
3. languages
4. to
5. a
6. thought
7. not
8. languages
9. He
10. saying, telling
11. he
12. the
13. was
14. country
15. that
16. very
17. a
18. ancient, interesting
19. it
20. in
21. large, big
22. to
23. take, row
24. not
25. he
26. a
27. boat
28. take, row
29. to
30. man, fisherman
31. across
32. him
33. you
34. the
35. know
36. need
37. just, only
38. you
39. said, answered, responded
40. life
41. fisherman, man
42. boat
43. from
44. lake
45. began
46. boat
47. water
48. over
49. the
50. how
51. do
52. If
53. how
54. fisherman, man
55. life
56. is
57. going

Unit 6.
AN HONEST ACTOR

1. in
2. He
3. room, bedroom
4. was
5. woman, lady
6. Jenkins
7. money
8. it
9. Jenkins
10. room
11. play, production, theater
12. closed
13. able
14. and
15. for
16. He
17. another
18. find
19. knew, believed, thought, suspected
20. to
21. his
22. the
23. call
24. asked, called, begged
25. to
26. from
27. on
28. up, all
29. clothes, belongings, things, possessions
30. his, one
31. suitcase, luggage
32. His
33. below, outside, downstairs
34. to
35. walked, went
36. out
37. his
38. towel
39. course
40. was, intended
41. He, Jack
42. beach, ocean
43. his
44. into
45. He, Jack
46. in, near
47. after
48. rich, wealthy
49. wanted, intended, planned
50. pay
51. that
52. first
53. recognize
54. new, smart, blue, etc.
55. she
56. Jack
57. My
58. thought, believed

Unit 7.
A CURIOUS BORDER GUARD

1. check, examine, inspect
2. border
3. people, drivers, travelers, tourists
4. into
5. Every, Each
6. Henry
7. factory
8. hill
9. a
10. bundle
11. top
12. the
13. stop
14. him
15. and
16. used
17. very
18. he
19. that
20. in
21. Then
22. the/his
23. it
24. ride
25. with
26. always
27. fine, expensive
28. items, things, trinkets
29. he
30. though
31. carefully, thoroughly
32. the
33. although
34. to
35. be
36. he, Henry
37. straw
38. worker's
39. he
40. to
41. that
42. the
43. me
44. you're
45. so
46. man
47. day
48. I'm
49. swear, promise
50. tell, call
51. confess, reveal, disclose
52. The
53. say
54. Then
55. to
56. Bicycles

Unit 8.
WORDS AND THEIR MEANINGS

1. a
2. go
3. her
4. every, each
5. she
6. In
7. was
8. held, had
9. Williams
10. much
11. Club
12. France, Holland, etc.
13. for
14. to
15. travel, go
16. and
17. so
18. But
19. able
20. had
21. her
22. came, arrived
23. were
24. did
25. care
26. Ms.
27. her
28. to
29. with
30. I
31. for
32. was
33. to
34. village, club
35. a
36. trip, vacation, holiday
37. arrived
38. the
39. first
40. several, many
41. language
42. bus
43. evening, night
44. town
45. of
46. to
47. They
48. where
49. soon
50. collected, gathered
51. to
52. about
53. heard
54. understood
55. to
56. voice
57. British

Unit 9.
A CREATIVE PAINTER

1. in
2. loved, liked, admired, enjoyed
3. chosen, selected
4. and
5. that
6. home, house
7. you
8. the
9. bedroom, room
10. a
11. decided
12. painted, decorated
13. the
14. to
15. the
16. thought, knew, believed
17. better, easier, faster
18. done, painted
19. Before
20. vacation
21. in
22. ashtray
23. much
24. paint, do, make
25. same
26. that
27. for
28. she

29. be
30. home, back
31. painter, worker
32. blue
33. and
34. he
35. match, obtain, get
36. But
37. home, back
38. ashtray
39. color, hue, shade
40. purple, clean, painted
41. the
42. happy, satisfied, content
43. painter
44. with
45. asked
46. very
47. clients, customers, people
48. Then
49. the
50. Do
51. it's
52. but
53. that
54. with
55. I

Additional Cloze.
PLASTIC: A FRIEND TURNED ENEMY

1. plastic
2. to, destroying
3. kills
4. seals, walruses
5. and
6. sea
7. spills
8. substances, products
9. plastics
10. the
11. scientists, environmentalists
12. on
13. during, in
14. were
15. Islands
16. Alaska
17. the
18. year, month
19. concluded, discovered
20. to
21. how, why
22. naturally, very
23. plastic
24. the
25. in
26. biologist, scientist
27. The
28. the, many
29. are
30. from
31. to
32. exhaustion, bleeding
33. efforts, struggle
34. The
35. themselves
36. of
37. have
38. of
39. made
40. rid
41. Plastic
42. strong, cheap
43. expensive, costly
44. strong, light
45. on
46. many, unfortunate
47. In
48. entwines, strangles, tricks, fools
49. is
50. litter, garbage
51. human, our
52. causing

Additional Cloze.
EDUCATION FOR DEMOCRACY: A POTENTIAL
AMERICAN EXPORT

1. students
2. These
3. San
4. variety
5. traditionally, long, always
6. function, rely, operate
7. punishment
8. approach, path
9. is
10. is
11. for
12. well
13. to
14. in, among
15. goal, objective
16. immediate, direct
17. children, students
18. learning
19. within
20. these
21. children's
22. as
23. learn
24. by
25. to
26. to
27. themselves
28. need
29. of, governing
30. believe, show
31. lies, is
32. their, individual
33. preach, dictate, condemn
34. children, youngsters
35. out
36. children
37. to
38. work, gather
39. such
40. peers, classmates, playmates
41. handle, respect
42. It
43. for
44. more
45. States
46. to
47. that, a
48. one, an
49. to
50. democracy
51. also
52. to
53. to
54. the

Additional Cloze.
SPACE: THE SILENT COMMUNICATOR

1. one
2. someone, somebody
3. the
4. inches
5. probably, softly
6. communication, message
7. change, variation
8. occurs, happens
9. audience, group
10. may
11. relationship, distance
12. member
13. in, to
14. in
15. When, If, Being
16. tend, try, prefer
17. as
18. separate
19. and
20. a
21. such
22. to
23. ranks
24. that
25. called
26. walked
27. over
28. as, particularly
29. may, then, immediately
30. this
31. communication, conversation
32. certain, sizable, considerable
33. more, most
34. themselves, them
35. On
36. American
37. It
38. situation, case, conversation
39. to
40. American
41. or
42. there
43. our, a
44. of
45. crowded, packed
46. to
47. normally, usually
48. in
49. a
50. is
51. for
52. therefore, always, usually
53. to
54. necessary
55. world, globe
56. increased, the
57. to
58. space, distance
59. Violations, Invasions
60. be
61. people's, different, specific
62. should, may, could, might
63. problems, difficulties